CHINA:
STATE CONTROL OF RELIGION

Human Rights Watch/Asia

Human Rights Watch
New York ● Washington ● London ● Brussels

ISBN: 1-56432-224-6
Library of Congress Catalogue Card Number: 97-77244

Human Rights Watch is dedicated to
protecting the human rights of people around the world.

We stand with victims and activists to prevent
discrimination, to uphold political freedom, to protect people from
inhumane conduct in wartime, and to bring offenders to justice.

We investigate and expose
human rights violations and hold abusers accountable.

We challenge governments and those who hold power to end
abusive practices and respect international human rights law.

We enlist the public and the international
community to support the cause of human rights for all.

HUMAN RIGHTS WATCH

Human Rights Watch conducts regular, systematic investigations of human rights abuses in some seventy countries around the world. Our reputation for timely, reliable disclosures has made us an essential source of information for those concerned with human rights. We address the human rights practices of governments of all political stripes, of all geopolitical alignments, and of all ethnic and religious persuasions. Human Rights Watch defends freedom of thought and expression, due process and equal protection of the law, and a vigorous civil society; we document and denounce murders, disappearances, torture, arbitrary imprisonment, discrimination, and other abuses of internationally recognized human rights. Our goal is to hold governments accountable if they transgress the rights of their people.

Human Rights Watch began in 1978 with the founding of its Helsinki division. Today, it includes five divisions covering Africa, the Americas, Asia, the Middle East, as well as the signatories of the Helsinki accords. It also includes three collaborative projects on arms transfers, children's rights, and women's rights. It maintains offices in New York, Washington, Los Angeles, London, Brussels, Moscow, Dushanbe, Rio de Janeiro, and Hong Kong. Human Rights Watch is an independent, nongovernmental organization, supported by contributions from private individuals and foundations worldwide. It accepts no government funds, directly or indirectly.

The staff includes Kenneth Roth, executive director; Susan Osnos, associate director; Michele Alexander, development director; Cynthia Brown, program director; Barbara Guglielmo, finance and administration director; Patrick Minges, publications director; Jeri Laber, special advisor; Lotte Leicht, Brussels office director; Susan Osnos, communications director; Jemera Rone, counsel; Wilder Tayler, general counsel; and Joanna Weschler, United Nations representative.

The regional directors of Human Rights Watch are Peter Takirambudde, Africa; José Miguel Vivanco, Americas; Sidney Jones, Asia; Holly Cartner, Helsinki; and Hanny Megally, Middle East. The project directors are Joost R. Hiltermann, Arms Project; Lois Whitman, Children's Rights Project; and Dorothy Q. Thomas, Women's Rights Project.

The members of the board of directors are Robert L. Bernstein, chair; Adrian W. DeWind, vice chair; Lisa Anderson, William Carmichael, Dorothy Cullman, Gina Despres, Irene Diamond, Fiona Druckenmiller, Edith Everett, Jonathan Fanton, James C. Goodale, Jack Greenberg, Vartan Gregorian, Alice H. Henkin, Stephen L. Kass, Marina Pinto Kaufman, Bruce Klatsky, Harold Hongju Koh, Alexander MacGregor, Josh Mailman, Samuel K. Murumba, Andrew Nathan, Jane Olson, Peter Osnos, Kathleen Peratis, Bruce Rabb, Sigrid Rausing, Anita Roddick, Orville Schell, Sid Sheinberg, Gary G. Sick, Malcolm Smith, Domna Stanton, Maureen White, and Maya Wiley.

CONTENTS

ACKNOWLEDGMENTS

This report by Mickey Spiegel is based on official Chinese documents, interviews in mid-1997 with individuals involved in religious activities in China and Hong Kong, and a wide range of secondary sources.

The report was edited by Jeri Laber and Sidney Jones. Tom Kellogg provided production assistance, and the Hong Kong office of Human Rights Watch gave important logistical support for much of the research.

The report is the latest in a series of Human Rights Watch reports covering freedom of religion in China and Tibet. They include *Freedom of Religion in China* (1992), *Religious Repression in China Persists* (1992), *Continuing Religious Repression in* China (1993), *Detained in China and Tibet: A Directory of Political and Religious Prisoners* (1994), *Persecution of a Protestant Sect in China* (1994), *No Progress on Human Rights (1994)*, *Religious Repression Persists* (1995), *Cutting off the Serpent's Head: Tightening Control in Tibet, 1994-1995* (1996), and *The Cost of Putting Business First* (1996).

This report would not have been possible without the assistance of numerous women and men who helped collect, confirm, and publicize information about many of the incidents described in this report. For their own security, we cannot mention them by name, but we are enormously grateful to them all.

I. SUMMARY AND RECOMMENDATIONS

Religion is becoming more and more important in China. In a country that remains officially atheist, conversions to Christianity have risen sharply, the country's 19 million Muslims are attracting the attention of their co-religionists elsewhere, and Buddhism is the fastest growing religion of all. The Chinese government acknowledges 100 million believers of all faiths out of a population of 1.2 billion, but it has been using the 100 million figure since the mid-1950s.

As interest in religion has increased, so has state control over religious organizations, in part because the Chinese government believes that religion breeds disloyalty, separatism, and subversion. Christianity and Islam in particular are seen as vehicles for foreign influence and infiltration by "hostile foreign forces," and religion is a critical element of the nationalist movements in Tibet and Xinjiang, where opposition to Chinese rule appears to be growing. Chinese authorities are keenly aware of the role that the church played in Eastern Europe during the disintegration of the Soviet empire. As a 1996 government document titled "Some Hot Issues in Our Work on Religion" illustrates, the Chinese government believes that Western countries are aiming to "achieve pluralistic political beliefs through pluralistic religious beliefs" and that they have used religion since the 1980s to subvert socialist countries.

Government control is exercised primarily through a registration process administered by the State Council's Religious Affairs Bureau through which the government monitors membership in religious organizations, locations of meetings, religious training, selection of clergy, publication of religious materials, and funding for religious activities. The government also now undertakes annual inspections of registered religious organizations. Failure to register can result in the imposition of fines, seizure of property, razing of "illegal" religious structures, forcible dispersal of religious gatherings, and occasionally, short term detention. In Tibet, control takes the form of political vetting of monks and nuns and strict supervision of their institutions.

While long-term imprisonment, violence, and physical abuse by security forces against religious activists still occur, they appear to be less frequent than they were at the time of the first Human Rights Watch study of religion in China in 1992. In 1997, we found isolated cases but no evidence of widespread or systematic brutality. When reports of these harsher measures do surface, they are increasingly denounced by central government officials as examples of the excesses of local officials and their failure to implement policy directives correctly. (It should be noted, however, that verifying reports of persecution and crackdowns remains very difficult, given restricted access to China.)

1

Every important Chinese leader and religious official has stressed that no one in China is prosecuted for his or her religious beliefs but rather for suspected criminal acts. Tightening of control over religion, they maintain, has come only at the expense of illegal groups and illegal activities. There are two problems with that argument, however. One is that refusal to register and submit to the kind of intrusive monitoring outlined above is precisely what renders an organization illegal. The second is that for Chinese officials, religious belief is a personal, individual act, and they distinguish between personal worship and participation in organized religious activities. It is the latter that they go to great lengths to control, not the former. The whole concept of religious freedom, however, involves not only freedom of the individual to believe but to manifest that belief in community with others.

The government's argument that its control of religion is strictly in accordance with the law is not new; it argues the same when confronted with protests over its treatment of political dissent. But several elements of its policy on religion have changed. While lessening its reliance on arrests and detention, the government is enforcing requirements on registration more strictly than ever before. It has narrowed the criteria it uses for identifying "authentic" religious groups, distinguishing between the five officially-recognized religions — Buddhism, Daoism, Catholicism, Protestantism, and Islam — and cults or sects practicing "feudal superstition." As illegal entities with no claim to protection, the latter are subject to a distinct set of penalties. Popular religion, a syncretic blend of Daoism, Buddhism and polytheistic elements that is central to the lives of millions of Chinese, is not even acknowledged as a religion. The government is also increasingly engaged in carefully planned mass campaigns promoting "socialist spiritual civilization" and inculcating patriotism as an antidote to religion. Political reeducation for the public at large is a prominent feature of the campaigns. Another new tactic is the government's increasing tendency to target the China-based representative of an "illegal" religious network (usually a foreign proselytizing organization) rather than individual members. It used to be that any local pastor or lay leader of an underground church linked to a foreign movement faced arrest; more and more, the Chinese government seems to be looking for an organizer at the district or provincial level.

In the kind of intrusive control the Chinese government exercises over religious activities, it violates the rights to freedom of association, assembly, and expression as well as freedom of religion. Article 19 of the Universal Declaration of Human Rights provides for the right to hold and express opinions and receive information and ideas "regardless of frontiers"; and Article 20 grants the right to peaceful assembly and association.

Article 18 of the Universal Declaration of Human Rights states:

Everyone has the right to freedom of thought, conscience and religion; this right includes freedom to change his religion or belief, and freedom, either alone or in community with others and in public or private, to manifest religion or belief in teaching, practice, worship and observance.

The only limitations that a government can impose, according to the declaration, are those necessary to secure "due recognition and respect for the rights and freedoms of others" and protecting "morality, public order and the general welfare in a democratic society." The peaceful gathering of unregistered groups is no threat to morality, public order, or general welfare; China's onerous registration requirements are clearly an unnecessary limitation on freedom of religion, particularly when failure to register results in some of the penalties outlined above.

China's narrow interpretation of freedom of religion as equivalent to freedom of private belief is contrary to the much broader international standard. In 1991, the U.N. General Assembly passed a resolution called "Declaration on the Elimination of All Forms of Intolerance and of Discrimination Based on Religion or Belief." The declaration in Article 6 elaborates on the right to religious freedom, noting that it includes the following elements:

a) to worship or assemble in connection with a religion or belief, and to establish and maintain places for these purposes;

b) to establish and maintain appropriate charitable or humanitarian institutions;

c) to make, acquire, and use to an adequate extent the necessary articles and materials related to the rites or customs of a religion or belief;

d) to write, issue and disseminate relevant publications in these areas;

e) to teach a religion or belief in places suitable for these purposes;

f) to solicit and receive voluntary financial and other contributions from individuals and institutions;

g) to train, appoint, elect or designate by succession appropriate leaders called for by the requirements and standards of any religion or belief;

h) to observe days of rest and to celebrate holidays and ceremonies in accordance with the precepts of one's religion or belief;

i) to establish and maintain communications with individuals and communities in matters of religion and belief at the national and international levels.

Thus, the Chinese government's distinction between legal and illegal religious activities based on either willingness to register with the Religious Affairs Bureau and accept government control or on the nature of the beliefs themselves (the five recognized religions as opposed to "sects") is a violation of freedom of religion. Its efforts to restrict organized religions activities, vet the selection of religious leaders and location of meetings, ban "unauthorized" materials, break up "illegal" gatherings, and hamper communication with co-religionists outside China are also in violation of this right.

In a place like Xinjiang, wracked by political violence, where China may have a legitimate concern about Islamic radicals from Afghanistan, Kashmir, or the Middle East providing military training and arms to Uighur separatists, Chinese authorities have reasonable grounds for arresting those suspected of violence or, under some circumstances, searching homes or religious institutions. A violation of religious freedom takes place, however, when people are forbidden to gather for prayers, when mosques deemed to be "illegal" because they are not registered are razed, or when the distribution of purely religious material is halted.

Recommendations

The People's Republic of China has not yet implemented many of the recommendations made by Abdelfattah Amor, the U.N. Special Rapporteur on Religious Intolerance, when he visited China in 1994. With a mandate to monitor the implementation of the 1981 U.N. Declaration on the Elimination of All Forms of Intolerance and of Discrimination Based on Religion or Belief, Amor reminded his Chinese hosts that the declaration, which is not a treaty but a statement of principles, recognizes both freedom of belief and the right to manifest that belief. Human Rights Watch believes religious freedom in China would be significantly enhanced if China carried out the Special Rapporteur's recommendations which included the following:

• amending Article 36 of the Chinese constitution, "so that the right to manifest one's religion is recognized along with the already recognized right to freedom of belief."

• adopting a text recognizing the right of freedom of belief and freedom to manifest that belief for all, including members of both the Chinese Communist Party and other socio-political organizations.

• adopting an explicit provision guaranteeing freedom of belief for those under eighteen years of age so as to ensure compliance with the

Convention on the Rights of the Child (ratified by China on March 2, 1992).

• ending surveillance of a kind that violates the right to freedom of belief and to manifest that belief.

• protecting the rights of those who hold "theistic beliefs" who may not be members of any officially recognized religion, in accordance with the 1981 Declaration.

• releasing anyone detained for membership in "unofficial" religious organizations or for other peaceful religious activities.

• carrying out human rights training, particularly on the subject of religious freedom, for state officials and judges.

Recommendations to the People's Republic of China:
• cease the practice of imposing administrative or criminal punishments against those who choose to worship outside the confines of government-approved mosques, monasteries, churches, temples, and meeting points.

• abolish the registration process in its current form so that it does not act as a tool to restrict peaceful religious practices.

• cease political vetting of religious personnel and, in Tibet, the practice of expelling those in monasteries and nunneries who do not meet political demands that infringe on their religious beliefs. All those expelled should be allowed to return promptly to their monasteries and nunneries.

• lift the ban on communication between monks and nuns in Tibet and the Dalai Lama.

• give unhindered access to the regions of Xinjiang and Tibet to foreign journalists and tourists.

Recommendations to the International Community:
• urge China to invite the U.N. Special Rapporteur on Religious Intolerance to return to China to assess progress toward implementation of his 1994 recommendations.

- include specific steps to increase freedom of association for religious groups as part of the broader agenda of human rights concerns discussed in the various bilateral human rights "dialogues" under way or scheduled between China and Japan, Australia, Canada, France, the European Union, and other governments. It should also be on the agenda for "summit" discussions of human rights concerns planned for later this year during the visits of Jiang Zemin to Washington and Ottawa, and Li Peng's scheduled visit to Tokyo in November.

- encourage visits from Chinese religious leaders to religious communities in other countries in order to exchange views on the problems of implementing a policy of religious freedom.

- include concern about China's restrictions on religious practices in a resolution at the U.N. Commission on Human Rights covering China's human rights practices more generally. Moves to sponsor and draft such a resolution should begin immediately.

- develop a coordinated policy for pressing China to open Xinjiang and Tibet to international human rights monitors and foreign journalists on a regular and unrestricted basis.

- discuss with the U.N. Committee on the Rights of the Child how best to negotiate the release of Gendun Choekyi Nyima, the eight-year-old child recognized by the Dalai Lama as the reincarnation of the Panchen Lama. The Chinese government has admitted to holding the child for "safekeeping."

II. THE THEORY: RELIGION MUST SERVE THE STATE

There is nothing trivial about religion. The management of religious problems is deeply concerned with politics, government policy and the masses....We must definitely adopt Lenin's attitude on such questions: "Be especially cautious," "Be most rigorous," and "Think things over carefully."
-- Ye Xiaowen, head of the Religious Affairs Bureau, March 14, 1996

Since early 1996, Chinese leaders, in government and party documents, speeches, and articles in official publications, have consistently reiterated the three guiding principles for management of religion: adaptation to socialist society, supervision according to the law, and correct and comprehensive implementation of the party's religious policy.[1] At the same time, they have made repeated reference to China's official atheism, its policy of separation of church and state, and the need for religion to serve economic development.

---

[1] The themes were set forth by Jiang Zemin, China's president and Chinese Communist Party secretary-general in November 1993 at a national conference on united front work. At the 1996 Fourth Plenum of the Eighth National People's Congress, Premier Li Peng echoed the same themes. He cited the 1982 State Council Document No.19, "Basic Viewpoint and Policy on the Religious Question During Our Country's Socialist Period," which offered a corrective to the Cultural Revolution policy of severe repression by advocating the cooptation of believers so they might serve socialist construction, and Document No. 6 of 1991, "Circular from Party Central and the State Council Concerning Certain Problems in Further Improving Religious Work." The latter was the first to mention adaptation, the first to espouse registration as a key supervisory mechanism, and the first to address the practical realities of implementing policy. Li Peng also referred to two 1994 sets of government regulations, No.144, "Regulations on the Supervision of the Religious Activities of Foreigners in China," and No.145, "Regulations Regarding the Management of Places of Religious Activity." On March 1, 1997 at the opening of the National People's Congress, Li Peng again made reference to the need for religious groups to adapt to socialist society.

7

Adaptation to socialist society

The Chinese government insists that religion must serve the state and adapt — or be adapted — to socialist society.[2] According to one analysis, this means highlighting moral teachings and curbing religious "extremism."[3] It also means a religion must adjust its "theology, conception, and organization" and interpret its canon and doctrine "in the interests of socialism."[4] According to Li Ruihuan, the Politburo member in charge of culture, this means that religious groups should help promote economic reform, or as a senior government official in Xinjiang put it, "Ancient traditions and religions cannot become obstacles to development."[5]

The principle of adaptation undermines freedom of religious belief by insisting that any principles and doctrines of the five recognized religions that do not conform to socialism should be changed. Expressions of faith that the government does not recognize as "normal" are subject to punishment.[6]

---

[2] For a thorough reassessment of the Chinese Communist Party's view of religion as a "complex social phenomenon," see Ye Xiaowen, "China's Current Religious Question: Once Again an Inquiry into the Five Characteristics of Religion, March 22, 1996. The article appeared in *Selection of Reports*, Party School of the Central Committee of the CCC, 1996, No. 5. A note at the end of the piece reads, *"Neibu (internal) issue* must be carefully kept and must not be reprinted without permission."

[3] "TSP/CC Pass Constitutions," *China News and Church Report,* March 14, 1997.

[4] "Some Hot Issues in Our Work on Religion," *Qiushi* editorial office publication, 1996, No. 5.

[5] "Government Official Stresses National Unity to China Religious Leaders," UCANEWS, February 22, 1996, *Tripod*, Volume XVI, No. 92, pp. 51-52. The Xinjiang leader's remarks appeared in "Vow to Curb Religion, Separatism," *South China Morning Post*, January 26, 1997.

[6] Article 36(3) of the Constitution of the People's Republic of China reads: "The state protects normal religious activities. No one may make use of religion to engage in activities that disrupt public order, impair the health of citizens or interfere with the educational system of the state." No definition of "normal" appears in any of the published regulations pertaining to religion, but in materials provided to Tibetan monks undergoing reeducation (see Appendix V), saying prayers or celebrating religious festivals is considered "normal" while "any action that is prompted by ignorance and superstition or that undermines the interest of the State and peoples' lives and property" is considered "irreligious."

Supervision according to the law

Increasingly the government is citing violations of Chinese law as its pretext for dismantling churches, monasteries, mosques, temples or congregations that refuse to adapt, especially targeting those individuals and organizations that attempt to operate outside official bureaucratic control.

The emphasis on law — including the Chinese constitution, the criminal code, and various administrative regulations and policies — to control religion is a relatively new development that emerged in the 1990s. Broadly worded laws, such as those on "counterrevolution," were, of course, in place long before and used against religious activists. But it was only in 1994 that a series of regulations on registration procedures for religious organizations and management of their activities was promulgated by the State Council.[7]

The emergence of these regulations may have been a response to what was seen by the government as a growing danger. It may have reflected an awareness on the part of the Chinese leadership that violence and force would neither succeed in preventing the growth of religion in China nor destroy religion's influence in society.[8] It may also have been designed to appeal to the international community, which had generally applauded China's tentative steps toward legal reform. But the government appears to have concluded as well that the regulations work, and that their enforcement is a feasible alternative to harsher methods of repression. The stress during the last two or three years thus has been less on punishment of individual offenders than on "lawful supervision" and strict regulation of religious organizations. There has been an emphasis as well on strengthening officially approved religious organizations and workers, with particular focus on the need to build up a younger generation of patriots.[9]

---

[7] See *Registration Procedures for Venues for Religious Activities,* Religious Affairs Bureau of the State Council, May 1, 1994; *Regulations on the Supervision of the Religious Activities of Foreigners in China's Borders*, Order of the State Council of the People's Republic of China, No. 144, January 31, 1994; *Regulations Regarding the Management of Places of Religious Activities*, Order of the State Council of the People's Republic of China, No. 145, January 31, 1994; *Method for the Annual Inspection of Places of Religious Activities*, Religious Affairs Bureau of the State Council, July 29, 1996, first published in *China Religion*, a quarterly publication of the RAB, Winter 1996.

[8] See "The Mystery Behind," *Tripod*, Volume XVII, No. 97, p. 43; "Church and State Relations In China: Characteristics and Trends: A Response," *Tripod*, Volume XV, No. 88, p. 20; Ye Xiaowen, "The Present State of the Religious Question in Our Country," Selected Reports from Party Central's Party School Series 100, No. 5, pp. 9-23.

[9] "Talk Policy, Talk Supervision and Talk Adaptation: The "Three Phrases" Must Be Thoroughly Implemented in Order to Do Religious Work Well," Ye Xiaowen's programmatic article published in *Renmin Ribao*, March 14, 1996; translated in *Tripod*,

This is not to suggest that the central government has succeeded in eradicating the use of extra-legal means to limit religious activity or that the laws in place are in accord with international human rights standards. But with surveys indicating that the faith of Chinese in the party and trust in a socialist future have declined, and with more and more people turning to religion, the government appears to be changing its methods of control and allowing its citizens to express their faith within the confines of the "law."[10] The laws themselves, however, are the problem.

Dangers of destabilization

The Chinese leadership argues that religion must "conduct its activities so as to safeguard the unity of nationalities and national unification[11] and resist "exploitation of religion by hostile domestic and foreign forces."[12] In 1991, well aware of the declining force of Marxism and the social dislocations brought about by economic reform, it launched a five-year "socialist spiritual civilization" campaign, with an emphasis on ideological education, patriotism, self-abnegation, dedication to the party, and rejection of bourgeois-liberal values. In November 1994, Zhao Puchu, president of the official Chinese Buddhist Association, noted at a seminar that by "guid(ing) everyone to set up correct ideals, convictions and beliefs, a world view, and a set of values," the party hoped to check discontent brought on by discrepancies in economic development and by the center's demands

---

Volume XVI, No. 95, pp. 44-51.

[10] In its May 7, 1997 edition, the magazine *Modern Ideological Trends* reported on results of surveys by the Communist Party Secretariat and the All-China Federation of Trade Unions. ("Party faith declines while religion rises," Reuter, May 6, 1997.)

[11] "Talk Policy, Talk Supervision...," p. 50. As part of his meeting with religious leaders during the 1996 Lunar New Year celebrations, Li Ruihuan stressed the role religious leaders must play in the important task of maintaining the unity of the nation and its various ethnic groups.

[12] "On Guiding Religion to Conform to Socialist Society," *Xinjiang Ribao*, June 11, 1996, in *Federal Broadcasting Information Service (FBIS)*, November 14, 1996."; "Communists Must Adhere to Marxist View of Religion," *Xinjiang Ribao*, May 21, 1996, p. 5, in *FBIS*, July 29, 1996.

on the provinces.[13] Zhao noted that "patriotic education" was the means for "inspiring the national spirit" so as to overcome obstacles and to "strengthen national cohesion."[14]

On August 11, 1996, Wang Zhaoguo, the director of Party Central's United Front Work Department, not only warned against splittism but inveighed against the use of religious issues by hostile international forces as "a breakthrough point" to "westernize" China.[15] While stressing that the religious situation in China was stable, he tied "recent" problems to changes in domestic and international relations. The same viewpoint was expressed in the same language in an article analyzing China's religious problem which appeared in 1996 in a restricted circulation (*neibu*) magazine, one of the publications of *Qiushi*, the Chinese Communist Party's official theoretical journal. Wang's remarks followed a ten-day conference in northeastern China at which religious leaders discussed measures to strengthen patriotism among believers and to replace the aging clergy and religious staff with young and middle-aged well-trained leaders. In May 1997, an article in *Tianfeng*, the magazine of the official Chinese Christian Church, called on all Chinese believers to see patriotism as their Christian duty.[16]

The danger that religion poses does not just come from the West in the view of Chinese leaders. On June 14, 1997, in a listing of seven factors that could destabilize the country, top party officials included "foreign radical religious forces (which) have greatly enhanced their influence in some areas occupied by minority nationalities."[17] One such area is Xinjiang Autonomous Region in the northwest, with a majority Muslim population and a good percentage of party members openly

---

[13] From a speech by Zhao Puchu, president of the official Chinese Buddhist Association, to a November 1994 seminar for religious leaders, parts of which are translated in "Political-Religious Issues in China Today," *Tripod*, 1995, Volume XV, No. 88, pp. 29-31.

[14] "Political-Religious Issues."

[15] "Religions Urged to Focus on Character," *China Daily*, August 13, 1996. Wang was reiterating the points Ye Xiaowen made in "Talk Policy, Talk Supervision...," pp. 44-51.

[16] "Can A Good Christian Be A Good Patriot, Too?" Amity News Service, June 1997.

[17] "CPC Circular Warns Against 7 Instability Factors," *Hong Kong Ming Pao*, June 14, 1997, in *FBIS*, June 17, 1997.

professing adherence to Islam.[18] The region, once known as East Turkestan, has an armed separatist movement led by members of the Uighur ethnic group. While the movement is primarily nationalist and not religious, the Chinese government believes the rebels are receiving support from radical Muslim groups abroad. The Xinjiang government chairman clearly believes religion and disunity are linked. "The biggest danger threatening stability," he said, "comes from separatism and illegal religious activities."[19]

Similar charges have been made with respect to Tibet, where the Chinese leadership has put a high priority on preventing collusion between the "Dalai clique" and "international reactionary forces." Again and again, Tibetan and Chinese officials accuse the Dalai Lama, Tibet's exiled leader, of using religion to engage in "political infiltration" and to sell his separatist ideas.[20] The Chinese government likewise views the Catholic church as a potential destabilizing force, given its role in the overthrow of communism in Eastern Europe. It is deeply suspicious of Protestantism, officially called Christianity in China, because of the overseas connections of its missionary organizations, not only to the West but to Taiwan and South Korea as well.

---

[18] See "Xinjiang Township Addresses Religion Among Party Members," *Xinjiang Ribao*, September 18, 1996, in *FBIS*, December 31, 1996. See also "Communist Party Members are Atheists--Investigation of Atheist Education in Turpan Prefecture," (*Xinjiang Ribao*, April 9, 1997, p. 6 in *FBIS*, June 20, 1997) for an account of in-depth atheist education in Turpan prefecture which featured "concentrated training," "mobile lecturing," "large-scale discussions," "individual talks," and "integrating education in atheism with tightening legal control over religion."

[19] "Vow to Curb Religion."

[20] "Dalai Uses Talks to `Pursue Separatism,'" *Xizang Ribao*, June 9, 1997, p. 3, in *FBIS*, July 24, 1997.

III. THE BUREAUCRACY: AN INSTRUMENT OF CONTROL

As early as the 1950s, the Chinese government began to set up an elaborate bureaucratic supervisory structure so that religion might better serve the political ends of the state.[21] With some shifts in emphasis, that structure remains. All key policy decisions are taken by the Standing Committee of the Politburo, the highest organ of the Chinese Communist Party. The United Front Work Department, a party organ, is responsible for implementing that policy. On the government side, the State Council's Religious Affairs Bureau (RAB), organized according to administrative levels with offices at the provincial, municipal, district and sometimes county levels, executes policy. Each of the recognized religions has a "patriotic association" to help manage the relationship between church and government, seeing to it that directives are implemented on the local level and that any relevant information is transmitted to the center. The structure of these associations parallels that of the RAB.

Catholicism and Protestantism have two monitoring bodies, one concerned with politics, the other more involved in ecclesiastical issues. The Chinese Catholic Bishops Conference, the leading national structure, is charged with implementing the "three-self" policy and approving the selection and ordination of bishops. The three-self policy, designed to remove foreign influence from religious affairs, maintains that all religious organizations should be self-administering, self-supporting, and self-propagating. The appointment of bishops goes to the heart of China's dispute with the Vatican, since it directly challenges the Pope's authority. The Chinese Catholic Patriotic Association (CCPA) is a mass organization of laity and clergy. Its purpose, under the leadership of the party and government, is to unite all Catholics in patriotism and to assist the Catholic Church in implementing the three-self policy.

All Protestants in China are united under one "post-denominational" church, on the theory that ideological, doctrinal, and ritual differences are secondary to the unity of Protestants insofar as patriotism and adherence to the three-self policy are concerned. The two organizations responsible for Protestant affairs are the China Christian Council (CCC), which is directly involved in internal pastoral affairs, and the Three-Self Patriotic Movement (TSPM), concerned with the relationships between individual churches and the Chinese government. According to its 1997 constitution, the TSPM's objectives are to foster patriotism

---

[21] For an organizational chart of the structure, see Human Rights Watch/Asia, "Religious Persecution Persists," *A Human Rights Watch Short Report*, vol. 7, no. 16, December 1995, p. 48.

among believers, strengthen unity among Christians, and protect church independence and autonomy. It is also charged with protecting the unity and stability of the nation and building spiritual and material civilization, all under the leadership of the Communist Party and the people's government.[22] According to one of its officials, the TSPM was not established to control Christianity's development but to defend it against imperialist control.[23]

In recent years, Chinese officials appear to have promoted the importance of the China Christian Council at the expense of the Three-Self Patriotic Movement, in part to assuage the historical antipathy of the Protestant community to the latter. Many believers suspect TSPM leaders of being atheistic, committed to promoting the party's interests rather than those of rank-and-file church members. In addition, believers resent the role the TSPM has played in persecuting congregations that have resisted registration. Church officials, on the other hand, stress the accomplishments of both organizations, such as arranging for Bible printing and distribution, helping negotiate the return of church property expropriated during the Cultural Revolution (1966-76), easing registration requirements, and bringing local level persecution to the attention of central authorities.[24]

Major splits have developed between the "official" or "open" and the "underground" Catholic churches and between the official or open Protestant meeting sites and so-called house churches.[25] Although there is no hard and fast line dividing the two sets of Catholics, members of the underground church recognize the authority of the Vatican, refusing either to register their churches or to obey the dictates of the Religious Affairs Bureau or the Chinese Catholic

---

[22] "TSP/CC Pass Constitutions."

[23] "Distortions About Christianity Refuted," Xinhua, June 9, 1997, in *FBIS*, June 10, 1997.

[24] "Running the Church Well: A Conversation with Bishop K.H. Ting," *Areopagus*, 1997, Volume 9, No. 4, p. 10. Bishop Ting headed both the CCC and the TSPM until December 1996. He is still president of Nanjing Seminary.

[25] "Official" is one of several terms applied to a registered church, mosque, temple, monastery, meeting point or other religious site; "open" is another. Non-registered Catholic congregations are often termed "underground" even though, in many cases, their existence is known to religious and Public Security Bureau officials. Unofficial Protestant meeting points are often labeled "house churches" even though the term is also applicable to registered sites and to congregations too large to meet in someone's home.

Patriotic Association. In some areas, the divisions are sharp and bitter; in others, official and underground clergy openly cooperate.[26] In some cases, members of the officially-recognized clergy have secretly made their peace with Rome.

On the Protestant side, the division is between established denominations, such as Anglicans, Methodists, Lutherans, Presbyterians, and Baptists, who have agreed to supervision by a lay bureaucracy and who aim to moderate Chinese religious policy by working from within the system, and a more conservative, aggressively evangelical wing. Those working from within the system are pushing for clear and comprehensive religious law. They argue that as the registration regulations have proven, a comprehensive law will protect them from arbitrary actions on the part of the state. It is far easier, they say, to fight for what is promised in writing.[27]

As vindication of their policy, they point to the growth in the number of Christian converts, although no one knows for certain how many there are.[28] (The late chairman of the Chinese Catholic Bishops Conference put the number of Catholics at 4 million, but the Holy Spirit Study Center in Hong Kong estimates that in 1996, China's Catholic population numbered 10 million.[29] Sources close to the China Christian Council estimate the number of Protestants at between 10 million and 13.3 million, but some estimates go up to 35 million and even higher.)[30]

---

[26] See Richard Madsen, "China's Catholics: Devout and Divided," *Commonweal*, April 25, 1997, pp. 14-16.

[27] From a statement made by the associate general-secretary of the China Christian Council to UCANEWS on July 11, 1997 ("China Seminaries Continue Inviting Outside Scholars Despite 1996 Regulation," UCANEWS, July 30, 1997).

[28] Comparative statistics are difficult to come by, and figures usually represent vested interests. Religious officials are reluctant to admit how fast the church is growing except when it suits their propaganda needs; official numbers count only registered worshipers and sites; other sources take into account clandestine congregants and explicitly acknowledge that all figures are estimates.

[29] "Estimated Statistics of Chinese Catholic Church, 1996," *Tripod*, Volume XVI, No. 96, p. 70.

[30] See "New Study Published on the Number of Christians in China," *China News and Church Report*, October 21, 1994; "China Protestants Could be as Many as 13.3 Million Protestant Group Says," UCANEWS, February 5, 1997.

Some aspects of the argument that working within the system creates space for growth, however, are flawed. To demonstrate growth, proponents compare current estimates of believers with the estimates from the Cultural Revolution period, a time when the government attempted to dismantle the entire religious infrastructure and persecute all believers. Moreover, much of the recent increase in numbers is attributable to the proselytizing efforts of conservatives willing to sabotage the government's "three-fix" policy that limits approved religious leaders to a fixed geographical location designated by the government. The evangelicals are much more wary of the registration process and of a legal system that remains tightly under the control of the party.

IV: THE PRACTICE: STATE CONTROL OF RELIGION

The most important mechanisms for controlling religion are registration of organizations, restrictions on what sites can be used for religious activities, and restrictions on personnel.

Registration

Registration has been China's most important means of supervising religious affairs since 1991 when Document No. 6, a party and government circular entitled "Concerning Certain Problems in Further Improving Religious Work," stated explicitly that "all sites of religious activities must be registered according to law" and that "the specific procedures will be laid down separately." To date there have been three such regulations issued. The January 1994 "Regulations Regarding the Management of Places of Religious Activity" laid out specific rules applicable to religious sites and to individual practitioners; the May 1994 "Registration Procedures for Venues for Religious Activities" detailed the exact process to be followed; and the 1996 "Method for the Annual Inspection of Places of Religious Activities" added the requirement that all religious sites had to be approved on an annual basis.

Ye Xiaowen, the conservative head of the government's Religious Affairs Bureau (RAB), reinforced the importance of registration in early 1996 at a party meeting for all provincial RAB directors. At the gathering, during which he outlined the direction religious work would take in 1996, he listed completion of registration for all religious sites as the first priority. "Our aim," he added, is not "registration for its own sake, but...control over places for religious activities as well as over all religious activities themselves."[31] According to China church watchers, even though registration was not completed by 1996 and the unpublicized new date is the end of 1998, the pressure to register has been fierce. One missionary summed up the impact when he complained, "There has never been a year like 1996 for canceling our training seminars for house church leaders — it has simply been too dangerous."[32]

---

[31] From Ye Xiaowen's special report at an RAB meeting on the direction religious work would take in 1996. On February 1, 1996, *People's Consultative Conference News* published the concluding segment in its "Religion and the Nation" section under the title "Stress Three Matters." See *Tripod*, Volume XVI, No. 92, pp. 45-50 for a translation of the piece.

[32] Reported in "Muslim Countries Dominate Persecution List," *Compass Direct*, February 21, 1997, p. 37.

By registering, congregations agree to certain limitations on their independence including control over selection of clergy, supervision of financial affairs, veto power over building programs and religious materials, and restriction on activities such as education and social welfare projects. Proselytizing among those under eighteen is strictly forbidden. RAB officials can, if they choose, examine church sermons for content. Among proscribed messages are those that preach about the second coming, judgment day, and the biblical account of creation. Membership rolls are made available to government authorities, and every individual in an official church requesting baptism must fill out a form in triplicate with photos attached. One form goes to the RAB, one to the relevant patriotic association, and the third to the work unit of the person baptized. Should one of the religious agencies object, the baptism cannot legally proceed.

The forcible replacement in 1994 of senior pastor Yang Yudong at Gangwashi, a large registered Protestant church in Beijing, by the powerful head of the Beijing Three-Self Patriotic Movement (TSPM) and China Christian Council (CCC) is a good example of official control over church personnel. Officials in the religious bureaucracy could not countenance Pastor Yang's tolerance of political dissidents. During the 1989 pro-democracy movement, a banner inscribed "Christians Support the Students" hung across the front of the church, and numerous dissidents attended services at Gangwashi. Officials were also unhappy with the church's steadily growing congregation — it attracted many young people in particular — and with the unofficial church outposts in Beijing's suburbs that Yang had established.

There are also less conspicuous examples of bureaucratic interference in the assignment of clergy to official churches. The eighty-year-old leader of a 1,500-member Protestant congregation in Guangdong province had proposed a candidate to succeed himself. In early February 1997, the local TSPM committee turned down his proposal, and there were no other candidates.[33] The Catholic community in the island province of Hainan has been without a priest since December 1996, but as of mid-May 1997, the Qingyuan city TSPM had not responded to requests that a priest be sent there.[34]

When Catholic or Protestant priests meet with foreign guests, they must often do so in the presence of patriotic association cadres or are later asked to give

---

[33] "Aged Town Church Leader Worries There Will Be No One to Succeed Him," UCANEWS, February 7, 1997.

[34] "China Priests Welcomed by Island Catholics; Encounter with Protestant Pastors," UCANEWS, May 14, 1997.

an account of their conversations. If official clergy have frequent contact with underground clergy, these same cadres will pressure them to report the details of the meetings.

The 1996 regulation mandating annual inspection of religious sites, which applies to all registered religious venues at the county level or above, also underscores the government's continuing reliance on registration as its chief management tool. Inspectors look to see that religious organizations are, among other things, conducting activities in accordance with national law and policy, maintaining a good financial situation, operating democratically, registering on time, and accepting annual inspection within applicable time limits. To establish compliance, local officials scrutinize all major religious and foreign-related activities including visitor lists, financial management, changes in conditions of registration, and changes and management of enterprises and properties. Those places that refuse inspection or fail to rectify the problems identified can be warned, ordered to cease their activities, or have their registration revoked.

Refusal to register no longer inevitably means arrest, however. In July 1996, municipal authorities in Beijing targeted Yuan Xiangzhen (Allen Yuan), a house church leader well known to religious and city officials, who had spent twenty-two years in a labor camp for refusing to join a patriotic association. His refusal to register had been overlooked in the interest of demonstrating China's benign religious policy. (A similar tolerance had been demonstrated in the case of one of China's best-known pastors in Guangdong, Samuel Lam.) The authorities had kept members of his congregation under close surveillance and did monitor church functions, but while they occasionally pressed Yuan to register, they generally left him alone. At the end of July, however, authorities ordered him to register or merge with either Gangwashi or Chongwenmen, two major Protestant churches in Beijing. These two churches not only were registered but had pastors closely linked to the local Religious Affairs Bureau. Finally, on August 7, after more visits by Public Security Bureau and RAB officials, the eighty-three-year-old preacher opted to end all Sunday services. Yuan continued pastoral visits and held services in city parks; he also held a youth meeting and a Bible class in his home. On March 9, 1997, a police officer asked that the Bible class be disbanded because it was illegal and "disrupted neighborhood harmony." Three participants were told that they had better worship at one of Beijing's larger churches. At the end of March, Yuan was told to keep the number of congregants down and not to let them stand in front of his house. To keep from being charged as a public nuisance, he prohibited singing during meetings.[35]

---

[35] *Bridge*, June 1997, No. 83, pp. 7-13.

In a case in suburban Jiaxing, Zhejiang province, which appears to have resulted from failure to register a religious site, the Religious Affairs Bureau detained three peasants for maintaining a "meeting point." The arrests of Sister Wu and the two others came on July 25, 1996. On October 11, two of the three received one-and-a-half-year "reeducation through labor" sentences; the third was administratively sentenced to a two-year term. All three were accused of "spreading evil propaganda to disrupt social order." The "meeting point" was not new; the three had maintained it at Dragon Bridge, Xincheng, for twenty years and had refused repeated requests by the prefectural RAB to join the Three-Self Patriotic Movement. On the evening of July 24, several hundred workers sent to the "meeting point" by the suburban RAB branch disrupted the meeting, confiscated the 100,000 *renminbi* (approximately US$ 11,000) building fund and all clothes, food, and other articles used in the church, and destroyed the eight meeting point houses. The three who were sentenced spent more than four months in the Beihua detention center. During that time, no mail reached the prisoners and postcards from the three were smeared so badly they could not be read.

Restrictions on religious places and personnel
Once a religious group has been vetted and registered, its members are still not free to engage in what they would consider normal religious activities. A series of central government regulations provides guidelines for determining what is "legal" and what is not; provinces, municipalities, counties, and other legal geographic jurisdictions have the authority to be even more restrictive when they issue implementing regulations. The November 30, 1995 "Regulations from the Shanghai Religious Affairs Bureau" are a case in point.

These regulations, which took effect on March 1, 1996, are comprised of sixty-three articles covering religious organizations, personnel, religious activities and where they can take place, religious institutes and properties, foreign contacts, and penalties for infringement. The document begins by acknowledging that the regulations are "formulated...to maintain lawful supervision over religious affairs..." (Article I) and that religious organizations "must...accept government supervision" (Article 11). In addition to the restrictions placed on organizations, personnel, and activities, the regulations require religious organizations "lawfully constituted" in Shanghai to "promote socialism, patriotism and education in government legal systems..." (Article 11). They end by vesting the power of interpretation in the Shanghai Religious Affairs Bureau (Article 62).

Penalties for "infringement" of the regulations can be severe. They progress from warnings and cease-and- desist orders to revocation of registration and confiscation of "structures, facilities...or income," to fines as high as 50,000 *renminbi* (approximately US$7,000) for organizations and 500 *renminbi* (approximately US$70) for individuals. Publication and distribution of religious materials is subject to "pertinent regulations" (Article 12), nowhere defined. Church-run business enterprises require approval (Articles 14 and 25) despite limitations on donations and the need to be self-supporting. Other articles require authorization for exhibitions or displays (Article 25), ban so-called superstitious activities (Article 28), limit the sites at which religious activities can occur (Article 29) and the persons authorized to perform public religious celebrations (Article 31), and ban religious debates (Article 32). Religious institutes such as seminaries are subject to similar strict regulation (Articles 35-39).

As for Shanghai religious personnel, they must be registered with the municipal Religious Affairs Bureau after having been vetted primarily by patriotic associations (Article 16). They cannot travel to other parts of China for religious purposes without approval from local religious organizations and registration at the municipal RAB. Religious visitors must follow the same procedure (Article 18). Foreign travel for religious purposes or invitations to foreign religious visitors are similarly subject to regulation (Article 48). The latter are expressly forbidden to "increase the number of believers among Chinese citizens" (Article 52).[36]

A set of local implementing regulations from Jingxian county in Hebei province dealing with rules for religious visitors from outside the county mandates even stricter controls. A guest must report to the entry and departure desk at the local Public Security Bureau (PSB), apply for temporary residence, and provide a copy of the application to the local Religious Affairs Bureau. After his departure, the hosting unit must submit a written report about the visitor's activities to both bureaus. As a precaution against unplanned events, an outsider who comes to visit friends or relatives or as a tourist also must notify the PSB and RAB of his or her planned activities. Visitors bringing money or gifts must first list their value and planned use in reports to those same bureaus. When the time comes for a donation actually to be put to use, an estimate of the total cost of the project must be submitted to both agencies and permission to proceed secured. A financial report of the project's income and expenses is required every six months.[37]

---

[36] See also "The Ningxia Hui Autonomous Region Has Strengthened Control Over Religious Affairs," *Ningxia Ribao*, July 29, 1997, in *FBIS*, August 11, 1997. The article specifically mentioned, "wanton construction of temples," the existence of sects, and the 250 religious sites whose loudspeakers interfere with "production, living conditions, and the work order of society."

[37] "Regulations concerning outside personnel who come to Jingxian (Hebei province) for activities, or bearing donations or gifts," *Tripod*, 1996, Volume XVI, No. 93, p. 58.

In addition to regulating places of worship and religious personnel, government bureaucrats supervise seminary education, (and see to it that it includes a large political component). They vet visiting religious scholars, and they approve candidates for religious study at home and abroad. According to several sources, an August 1996 internal document for use by the Religious Affairs Bureau and other religious institutions tightened conditions for seminaries wishing to invite foreigners, including Hong Kong residents, to teach. Before August 1, visiting theologians could teach in seminaries as long as a bishop or seminary official issued an invitation and the local RAB approved. Since August 1996, permission must be obtained from the State Education Commission of the State Council as is required of all Chinese universities and technological institutions. The Chinese Catholic Bishops Conference and the Chinese Catholic Patriotic Association (CCPA) did ask central authorities to take into account the special circumstances of seminaries but apparently to no avail. According to Liu Bainian, vice-chairman of the CCPA, as of July 14, 1997, the official Catholic Church had not even discussed how to implement the decree.

Implementation of the regulation is a good example of how decrees from central authorities are applied to local jurisdictions. The document itself has had limited circulation and has been enforced differently in different provinces. In Shaanxi province, the rector at Xi'an seminary stated that he did not even know about the new regulation.[38] By contrast, in Wuhan, Hubei province, it apparently has been strictly enforced, especially in relation to priests and others from Hong Kong holding home visiting permits. In either February or March 1997, Father Thomas Law, who had been at Wuchang seminary only a few days, was asked to leave immediately because the school allegedly had not obtained the necessary permit. Father Law had taught in mainland seminaries for some seven years before his arrival at Wuchang.

Study abroad has also become more difficult. Even though a program has been in effect for religious students for almost a decade, the numbers of approved candidates, which had been rising, dropped precipitously during 1995 and 1996.[39] Many students who apply to the RAB and the Justice Ministry for passports after they have been accepted by institutions abroad and even offered scholarships are turned down without explanation.

---

[38] "China Seminaries Continue Inviting."

[39] "Selection Important as Fewer Seminarians Study Abroad," UCANEWS, March 5, 1997.

Religious publishing

Religious publishing is also strictly controlled.[40] The Shanghai Guang Qi Research Center (GQRC), China's largest Catholic publishing house, had to wait for government approval before it could begin publication of the *New Catechism of the Catholic Church in China*.[41] The delay had to do with negotiating a compromise on the use of certain terms and finding a way around the chapter on abortion. The GQRC, which supplies printed materials to Catholic churches throughout China, also needed official permission to expand its operation. Its publications may only be distributed in certain, authorized outlets.

Protestants face the same restrictions. The Chinese Christian Council determines the number of authorized Protestant Bibles to be printed and sells them through fifty centers at about half cost. By June 1997, the fully licensed Amity Printing Company had produced some 15 million Bibles, but local shortages mean that unregistered church members sometimes have difficulty obtaining them.[42]

Suppression of the Catholic underground

As noted above, the Catholic organizations and congregations that continue to recognize the authority of the Vatican constitute the Catholic underground. Officials are determined to narrow the space within which the underground can maneuver and make use of a variety of means to do so, including mass campaigns, surprise raids, and imposition of fines apparently designed to bankrupt the underground church.

Cooperation between the district party secretary, the public security chief, and officials from the Religious Affairs Bureau resulted in the detention of at least eighty and possibly as many as 120 members of underground Catholic churches near Linchuan city, Fuzhou district, Jiangxi province, beginning on November 14, 1996. The preemptive strike appeared to be an attempt to stop local underground members from congregating on Yujia mountain on Christmas Day. The mountain had become the site of gatherings of thousands of people on important Catholic feast days, and the gatherings were frequently subject to raids. Forty-two of those initially detained in the November 1996 strike have been identified. According to

---

[40] "Some Hot Issues."

[41] "Publication of New Chinese Version of Catechism Targeted in 1997," UCANEWS, February 4, 1997.

[42] "Protestant Bible Hits 15 Million, China Distribution First in World," UCANEWS, June 3, 1997. By August the figure quoted was close to 20 million.

a Religious Affairs Bureau official in Linchuan, the detained Catholics were "not arrested but sent to attend 'learning classes.' And they were all released."[43] Other sources report that Chinese authorities extracted stiff fines, in some cases amounting to a half year's income, before permitting releases, but that at least some of those detained may have been still in detention as of September 5, 1997. The exact number, their identification, and the fate of the other November 1996 detainees are unknown.[44]

Less than a week after the November 1996 incident, a seven-month "united" campaign began in nearby Donglai township, Chongren county, Fuzhou district, ostensibly to curb the "illegal" activities of the underground Catholic church, to strengthen the administration and standardize the conduct of religious activities, and to promote social stability. According to a document issued by the Donglai Township Committee of the Chinese Communist Party outlining a staged action plan, the growth in the Catholic population was attributable to "intensified infiltration by hostile religious forces and elements outside our borders and unlawful activities of underground religious forces."[45] The campaign's aim, therefore, was to stop all "illegal" activities, force believers in the villages of Donglai, Shanbei, and Leifang, among other areas to join the official church, crush the Catholic underground network, and cut off local "illegal" elements from foreign contacts. According to the document, the involved officials and team members were to "handle political issues as non-political issues, and religious issues as non-religious issues."

To accomplish their ends, the Donglai Communist Party branch initiated a strategy of "transformation through education, divide and disintegrate, unite with the majority and attack the few." During the preparatory phase, the county's "workforce" was to be combined into "spiritual civilization propaganda force" teams to be stationed in recalcitrant villages, and a propaganda campaign to target different groups of underground clergy, core elements, and the mass of believers was to be designed and "customized."

---

[43] "Government Curbs Underground Catholics in Villages of Jiangxi Province," UCANEWS, January 20, 1997.

[44] For details on detentions in 1994 and 1995, see "Religious Persecution Persists.""

[45] Document made available by the Cardinal Kung Foundation, Stamford, Connecticut.

Teams were required to visit every family and make friends among the villagers. Then, with the help of the police, they were to set up files on every member of the local and transient populations. Team members had to undertake particular study of certain targeted groups, including clergy, believers within the government, the party, and other communist organizations, and those responsible for "illegal activities." The study involved an effort to understand their "activity schedules, overseas connections, the degree of stubbornness, the traits that could be taken advantage of, and their psychological characteristics."

During the first half of December 1996, party members, young activists, underground clergy, and leaders were required to study religious policies, laws, and regulations and the national spiritual civilization drive. The need to "unify the thoughts" of party members so they could become strong enough models to counter the influence of the underground was, in fact, "the first objective." The creation of "a reserve force of zealous young people" to help the party was another prime objective. The reeducation class directed at clergy and core elements aimed to indoctrinate them in party policy and objectives and to make them aware of activities that were "unreasonable and illegal." Only a few "stubborn" and core underground members were to be "strictly controlled."

Other measures, all deemed legal, called for first sealing minor centers of illegal religious activities, then registering and reopening them; isolating believers and forcing them to sign confessional statements accepting the official church; thoroughly destroying any underground monastery or convent that could be located; and eliminating any large scale illegal assemblies such as those anticipated on Christmas. To accomplish the latter, residents were to be warned that they could not leave their home villages nor were they allowed to have visitors. Exits were to be blocked, and licenses for vehicles and equipment used for religious purposes were to be revoked and their users fined.

Authorities paid particular attention to proselytizing among minors, calling for infiltration of schools and strict punishment for students carrying religious materials and teachers performing illegal religious activities. Interference with other government directives on the pretext of religion, such as family planning policies, was also to be dealt with firmly but on a case-by-case basis. The final consolidation phase called for setting up a permanent religious surveillance group for the villages.

Among the ten propaganda slogans listed in the Donglai document, one banned gatherings on Yujia mountain and warned that violators would be "severely" punished. Others banned the "hosting" of religious visitors or the offering of sites or supplies for illegal activities; such actions would result in severe punishment. Other slogans referred to "criminal activities committed in the name of religion" and "illegal missionary activities."

To date, no information about actual implementation or the results of the campaign are available.

The Jiangxi document is only one of several that illustrate the government's methods of religious control. Another comes from Baoding diocese, northern Hebei province, another stronghold of underground church activity. In this case, the information comes from an appeal letter to the government of the People's Republic of China dated June 15, 1996. The letter is signed by Bishop Su Zhimin, the underground bishop of Baoding diocese. It details not only a well-planned operation that had started six months earlier but considerable abuse as well.

In his letter, Bishop Su asked the Standing Committee of the National People's Congress to investigate the "serious unlawful encroachment on the citizens' rights and to administer corrective measures." The letter detailed how, starting in April 1996, "task forces from the city and county government, under the guise of helping Catholics escape from poverty," used economic and social sanctions, such as suspension of retirement benefits and loss of working permits, as well as force, to "persuade" Catholics to renounce allegiance to the underground church. Some 4,000, almost 10 percent of the Catholic population, did so. Of the total, three quarters were under eighteen years of age. To accomplish their ends, work teams arranged to have school children expelled, teachers dismissed, round-the-clock study groups substituted for field work, and residents confined to their villages. In one village, Da Hou, inhabitants had to report in eight times a day and were fined 100 *renminbi* (US$12) if late. Believers were required to sign a "Certificate of Warranty," actually a renunciation pledge, guaranteeing that the signatory would abide by official religious policy, avoid all contact with underground clergy, and oppose the infiltration of foreign religious powers, i.e., the Vatican. According to Bishop Su, in two villages, Nansong and Nanmanying in Qingyuan county, many of those who refused were tortured.

The authorities targeted buildings as well as people, authorizing armed police to tear down or seal churches and "prayer houses." In Quankun village, some 300 armed police were deployed to close the village church. Another church was converted to a kindergarten. Even a home for the elderly in Tiangezhuang was forced to close. In May 1996, as part of the same effort, Bishop Su continued, Chinese authorities took extraordinary measures to end what had been an annual month-long pilgrimage to a Marian shrine in the village of Donglu. Many of the details are still not known, but it seems clear from other sources that despite roadblocks, people did succeed in entering Donglu and that at the height of the tension, police deliberately demolished at least part of the shrine. Cui Xingang, the parish priest in Donglu, has been in and out of detention since his initial arrest in

May 1996. At last report, in June 1997, he had again disappeared.[46] Secular authorities took it upon themselves to decide what was, or was not, holy. They argued, "There is no foundation for asserting that Donglu is a so-called sacred place and therefore cannot be venerated as such."[47]

Bishop Su himself went into hiding for seventeen months after the Donglu crackdown. He was reportedly taken into custody on October 8, 1997 in Xinji, Hebei province and returned to Baoding under public security bureau escort.

Evidence of mass campaigns came also from northern Zhejiang province in the form of a March 1, 1997 secret document (No. 19) from the Tongxiang Municipal Committee of the Chinese Communist Party. The document indicated that the campaign outlined in an earlier internal (*neibu*) document, dated February 27 and entitled "Opinion Concerning Carrying Out the Special Struggle to Curb the Illegal Activities of Catholic and Protestant Christians According to the Law," had been approved by the Tongxiang municipal government. Both documents were circulated to the party committees and governments of the villages and townships and to departments of various municipal organs, factories, and mines directly under municipal authorities.

The February 27 document was a product of the municipal-level Public Security Bureau and the United Front Work Department. Its language lends some credence to the assertion that local campaigns are mounted in response to higher level directives. After declaring that Tongxiang had already "embarked on the course of working within the legal framework" to implement the party's policy toward religion, it goes on to claim that the municipality had to extend its efforts because "infiltration and subversive activities on the part of outside hostile forces that use religion as a means to 'westernize' and 'divide' our country had increased." The language almost duplicates that used by the director of Party Central's United Front Work Department in an August 1996 speech, as well as the language in "Some Hot Issues in Our Work on Religion." The Tongxiang document went a step further in expressing alarm at "contacts" established between Catholics and Protestants.

There is also evidence from the document that Tongxiang officials planned to use other laws to "supervise" religious activities, including the Law on Assembly and Demonstrations to crack down on large-scale meetings, assembly

---

[46] For additional details on events in Hebei, see Human Rights Watch/Asia, "The Cost of Putting Business First," *A Human Rights Watch Short Report*, Volume 8, No. 7 (C), p. 19.

[47] Private communication, June 1997, Hong Kong.

sites, and training classes; urban construction and land codes to close down churches; and laws governing printing and publishing to restrict dissemination of religious material. From the repeated mention of "criminal" activities in the February 27 document, it is reasonable to assume that China's criminal law will also be invoked.

The Tongxiang campaign is reminiscent of that in Donglai. It established a special party-led team with offices located in the municipal Public Security Bureau to coordinate the effort. At the township level, it mandated work teams composed of recruits from public security; the united front department; government offices of religion, propaganda, civil affairs, and education; the procuratorate, the courts; city construction agencies; and trade union, youth, and women's organizations. Authorities identified three major problems. The first, the "three struggles," referred to competing for influence with "self-styled missionaries" who used "such illegal methods as making house calls and visiting the hospitals" to win followers; competing for members against house churches which "set up meeting places close to the open churches;" and competing for influence between different recognized religions and between different denominations. According to the February 27 document, the other two identified major problems, the existence of three churches not under official control and sixteen smaller unregistered "sites," "adversely affected the building of socialist spiritual civilization and social stability." In addition, the document declared that the problem of minors and party members becoming believers had to be addressed.

As a counter to this, the document recommended isolating missionaries and influential figures from the general populace, strengthening the daily supervision of religious affairs, pushing ahead with registration, shutting down illegal sites, and persuading Christians to switch allegiance to government-controlled congregations, thus promoting divisiveness within both the Protestant and Catholic communities. The entire effort was to last through June 1997. No information about the effects of the campaign are available.

The February 27 document proposed that after the work teams thoroughly understood the underground and missionary forces and had collected legally valid evidence, they should embark on an in-depth education campaign coupled with more forceful measures. For example, "illegal assembly sites...should be...put under long-term control of the local police stations and public security committees," and underground bishops and priests and "self-styled" missionaries who "cannot yet be punished according to the law," should be "placed under strict surveillance." Finally, the document makes clear the secret nature of the work, warning the news media not to report on the campaign.

In contrast to the carefully planned campaigns, the Public Security Bureau also makes use of unannounced raids on unregistered sites and unofficial personnel. In Shanghai, for example, public security officers made two raids a month apart on clergy connected to the Catholic underground. In the first raid, on March 4, 1997, eight agents in a three-and-a-half-hour search confiscated Bibles, rosaries and other religious articles, and 20,000 *renminbi* (approximately US$2,400) from the home of eighty-one-year-old Coadjutor Bishop Fan Zhongliang, an underground church leader and a veteran of more than twenty years in Chinese labor camps.[48] At the time, the Public Security Bureau, as it always had, was maintaining a close watch on the bishop's activities, including monitoring the Sunday services in his house. Bishop Fan had been saying mass at home every Sunday, at first to hundreds, and from March 1996 on, to less than twenty-five, in hopes of avoiding police interference.

In the second instance, a five-hour raid at the home of Father Zen Caijun, which began on the night of March 29 and lasted into March 30, 1997, Easter Sunday, netted more religious articles, cash, a telephone, a video recorder and other electronic equipment.[49]

Fewer details are available about a police search that same month at the home of underground Bishop Xie Shiguang in Fu'an, Fujian province, only that money and religious books were confiscated.[50] But earlier, in June 1996, Public Security Bureau officers searched the Fu'an church and confiscated tens of thousands of US dollars. When no explanation was given for how the church came to have such a large amount of foreign currency, auxiliary Bishop Huang Shoucheng and two priests were held for several hours, then sent home. That same evening, Bishop Xie fled to the countryside and hid for several weeks before venturing back to Fu'an. A year later, the money had not been returned, and church leaders and government officials were still negotiating. Part of the government's

---

[48] Bishop Fan was ordained a Jesuit priest in 1951 and a bishop in 1980. He has been in charge of the underground church in Shanghai since 1988 when Cardinal Gong Pinmei, then eighty-six, left China for the U.S.

[49] According to March 23 and April 1, 1997 press releases from the U.S.-based Cardinal Kung Foundation, no receipts were issued and no reasons for the intrusions given.

[50] Human Rights Watch interview, June 1997, Hong Kong.

interest in Bishop Xie is in learning more about the underground in all of Fu'an county and the surrounding area.[51]

Suppression of cults

One of the tactics by which the government limits religious organizations is by labeling some groups as cults or sects rather than as legitimate offshoots of any of the five officially recognized religions.[52] A Public Security Bureau circular, issued sometime between April and August 1996, revealed that the central government had authorized a crackdown on rural cults.[53] The document specifically mentioned the "counterrevolutionary" Shouters (*Huhan Pai*), a Protestant group.[54] But other persecuted groups include the "counterrevolutionary" Daoist *Yi Guan Dao* and the Buddhist Self-Nature Association;[55] the Blood and Water Holy Spirit, an "illegal infiltrating organization" founded by visiting Christians from Taiwan;[56] the heretical Lingling, Wilderness (*Kuangye Hui*), and Disciples (*Mentuhui*); and groups such as the Born Again (*Cong Sheng*). An internal article puts the number

---

[51] Bishop Xie, now in his late seventies, had been arrested on July 27, 1990 along with nine others at a meeting on church affairs in Xiapu diocese and was released on January 28, 1992. Premier Li Peng reportedly told then President George Bush that the bishop and priests had breached Chinese law but had shown repentance.

[52] In Chinese, "cult" is rendered as "perverse religion," and "sect" as "heresy" (*Bridge*, August 1997, No. 84, p. 2).

[53] "New Attempt to Crack Down on Cults," *China News and Church Report*, September 6, 1996.

[54] Human Rights Watch/Asia, "The Persecution of a Protestant Sect," *A Human Rights Watch Short Report*, June 1994, Volume 6, No. 6.

[55] In late July 1996, police raided the headquarters of the one hundred-member Self-Nature Association headquartered in Nan county, Hunan province, confiscating name lists, flags, badges, and religious books and seizing two leaders, Hu Songhai and Xiong Tianyu. According to police allegations, the group was a reactivation of the Ancient Buddhist Hall which had previously been branded counterrevolutionary (China in Transition column, *Far Eastern Economic Review*, August 29, 1996).

[56] The cult's full name is the Jesus Christ Blood and Water Holy Spirit Full Gospel Preaching Team. "Illegal infiltrating organisation" refers to an overseas group that entered China illegally and plans to carry on activities that the Chinese government deems illegal.

of cultists at 500,000 spread across most provinces, autonomous regions, and municipalities (Beijing, Shanghai, Tianjin, and Chongqing) and advocates that severe measures be taken.[57] It charges members with raving about breaking down central control in rural areas where party domination is weak, and raising the slogan, "seize church power first and then take over the political power." The document goes on to accuse members of sabotaging production, creating "social panic," and undermining "social order."

As regards some of the alleged cults, mainstream Christian doctrine holds that the belief structure and/or means of expressing faith are heterodox and undermine the integrity of religious doctrine. Examples include one group's stricture that salvation can only come through membership in that particular assembly; belief that only certain practices, such as continual weeping for several days and nights, can earn salvation; a leader's proclamation that he is the savior returned or that the date of Judgment Day is set and known. Chinese authorities then seize on the heterodox label to prove the illegality of the alleged cult or sect, marking its practices as "feudal superstition" rather than religious expression. In many instances, they make little or no attempt to differentiate between so-called cults and unregistered house churches.

Religious Affairs Bureau head Ye Xiaowen singled out cults that "seriously threatened social and political interests" as unlawful. He went on to say, "Most of the ringleaders were pleasure seekers who hated work. They distorted religious doctrines, created heresy...and attempted to overthrow the government; or they also used superstitious beliefs to fool the people...or they had group sex, raped women, and defrauded people's money."[58]

It is difficult, if not impossible, for outsiders to verify or refute the accusations. As one informant explained, "If they meet in the dark, they get accused of rape."[59] Another explained, "When we try to collect a tithe, we are accused of trying to cheat people or amass wealth. When we preach that 'there is hope in this world so we believe in God,' the government says it means that it (the government) is hopeless and we want to overthrow it."[60]

---

[57] "Some Hot Issues."

[58] "Further on PRC Refuting `Slander' on Religious Freedom," Xinhua, June 10, 1997, in *FBIS*, June 11, 1997.

[59] Human Rights Watch interview, May 1997, Hong Kong.

[60] Human Rights Watch telephone interview from New York, May 1997.

The March 16, 1997 arrest of Xu Yongze,[61] leader of the Born Again movement, raised alarms throughout the Christian evangelical community in the U.S. when it was reported erroneously that he was slated for execution.[62] At least seven others were arrested with him in Zhengzhou, Henan province, a center of the evangelical movement in China. Some of those seized were active in unity talks that had been taking place since November 1996 among leaders of house church movements. The Shouters, labeled heterodox by the orthodox Christian community, and the True Jesus and Born Again movements, were among those represented. On May 20, Xu reportedly was transferred to an unknown location, and on September 25, he was reportedly sentenced to a ten-year term by the Zhengzhou Intermediate Court. Of the other seven arrested, Xu's wife, Qing Jing; Qin Musheng and his older brother; and a woman called Sister Fengxian were believed to be still in detention as of October 1997. The status of three others, Wang Xincai, a Shouter from Lushan county, Henan,[63] Elder Qiao and Brother Sun remained unclear. A ninth detainee, Hsu Chu-chun (Xu Zhujun), a Taiwanese woman now a U.S. citizen, was interrogated and released.

The Protestant community both inside and outside China is divided as to whether the Born Again movement is heterodox. Chinese religious authorities insist it is, because the three-day crying period that is required before a penitent is considered to have repented, been reborn, and saved does not fit with orthodox practice. Han Wenzao, president of the Chinese Christian Council, went so far as

---

[61] Xu Yongze, now in his mid-fifties, from Zhenpeng country, Henan, had been free but under surveillance or in hiding after his release from a re-education camp in April 1991. Starting as an itinerant preacher in 1968, he was one of a group of evangelists responsible for the revival of the house church in Henan province. Wang Xincai, Qin Musheng, and Liu Fenying were three of his early followers. In August 1982, Xu was arrested at a bus stop as he waited for them to return from an evangelical trip to Sichuan province. Sent to a labor camp, he managed an escape but waited three years before resuming his own travels and his training of evangelicals who then went on to proselytize in virgin areas, especially the border regions of Inner Mongolia, Xinjiang, Tibet, Qinghai, Yunnan, and Guizhou. By 1988, Xu was back in a labor camp serving a three-year administrative sentence. For additional details see Human Rights Watch/Asia, *Detained in China and Tibet: A Directory of Political and Religious Prisoners*," (New York: Human Rights Watch, 1994), p. 403.

[62] The execution of Wu Yangming, another "cult" leader, lent a certain amount of credence to the report.

[63] Wang Xincai was released some time after 1994 from a fifteen-year term imposed on June 2, 1984. His original release date was June 1, 1998. For additional details see *Detained in China and Tibet...* and "Persecution of a Protestant Sect."

to say that "Xu is not a Christian at all"; and that his detention was in accordance with the "Regulations on the Registration and Administration of Social Organizations."[64] Han insisted that Xu "poisoned people's minds by spreading the views that 'the end of the world is coming, and disasters are falling down,' illegally gathering and instigating people to do no normal work but cry collectively every day. Many people became distraught and could not cope with their own life. And the normal life and production of local people were also seriously affected." Han went on to contend, "The detaining of Xu is definitely not persecution of Christians by the Chinese government, but a normal handling of criminal persecution," comparable to the United States and Japanese measures against the Branch Davidians and the Aum Shinrikyo respectively.

The *Jiangxi Legal News* reported a crackdown against the Blood and Water Holy Spirit in 1996.[65] On May 9, 1996, public security officers in rural Xinjian county, Jiangxi province, shut down the sect, took what the newspaper called "lawful measures" against its leader, Zhang Guihua, and required her twelve followers to undergo a course of "intensive education and study" and to sign "certificates of repentance." According to the report, sect members did promise to cease their "illegal activities," including the distribution of Bibles and "attacking and denigrating the religious policies of the Communist Party." Zhou Zuoyun, the first local leader of the Blood and Water Holy Spirit, was administratively sentenced to a two-year "re-education through labor" term in 1993 and reportedly was on the run after his release in January 1995.

Suppression of evangelists and overseas missionaries
The government's demand that church leaders be assigned to one location and that their activities stay within a fixed geographic sphere, conditions that have to be met for registration to be approved, effectively proscribes all evangelical activities.[66] Religious officials use the edict to try to curb the activities of indigenous evangelists. In April 1997, in Wenzhou City, Zhejiang province, and the surrounding rural area, as many as 200 evangelical leaders were detained. In an unusual move, police rounded up the leaders one by one. They were not picked up

---

[64] "Christian Council President Comments on 'Persecution,'" Xinhua, June 23, 1997, in *FBIS*, June 24, 1997.

[65] "Christian Group Said Targeted in 'Strike Hard' Campaign," *Eastern Express*, June 28, 1996, in *FBIS*, July 2, 1996.

[66] "Registration Procedures for Venues for Religious Activities," Article 2.

in the usual fashion, that is during a police raid on a religious meeting when everyone present who cannot manage to escape is seized. At least one leader was still in custody as of May 10, the others were released after paying fines averaging 500 *renminbi* (approximately US$60), an exorbitant amount by rural standards. Such fines are designed to bankrupt a locality's missionary network.

Three police raids in three and a half months on a house church in Xiangshan, Huadu, Guangdong province, are illustrative of attempts to crush a missionary network. During the first, on March 15, 1996, all the chairs and Bibles were confiscated. The books had been printed by the officially licensed Amity Press in Nanjing. In this case, an overseas ministry had supplied the Bibles to the church. During the raid, worshipers were subject to body searches. In the second raid, on June 21, police took chairs and Bibles that had replaced those taken in the first raid, as well as tables and a tape recorder. They seized Yang Qun, at whose home the meeting was in progress, and his seventeen-year-old son, Jiang Guoxiong. They confiscated the latter's money and watch but issued no receipt. A week later, thugs reportedly hired by the police interrupted the meeting, took bedboards and new Bibles, and told the participants that if they continued to meet, excrement would be spread all over the house and the believers. By the end of August, Jiang had been released, the house church was still meeting, but electricity to Yang's home had been cut.[67] Human Rights Watch was not able to determine whether Yang Qun had also been released.

On August 25, 1996, a Chinese official formally asked his Republic of Korea (ROK) counterpart to put a stop to the large numbers of illegal Korean missionaries operating in Jilin, Heilongjiang, and Liaoning provinces in northern China disguised as businessmen or teachers.[68] Local government officials, as opposed to those in Beijing, are more reluctant to expel the missionaries, as they are appreciative of the amount of economic activity Koreans generate within the region.

The Korean government agreed to try to meet the request from Beijing. According to the ROK Foreign Ministry, in December 1996, four missionaries

---

[67] "Jiang Guoxiong Released," *China News and Church Report*, August 23, 1996.

[68] "China Tells South Korea to Stop Sending Missionaries," *China News and Church Report*, September 6, 1996. See also, "Vigilance Against Infiltration by Religious Forces from Abroad," a 1990 internal document which has a section dealing with South Korea's infiltration of border areas (Human Rights Watch/Asia, *Freedom of Religion in China* (New York: Human Rights Watch, 1992, p. 56).

were detained and held for a week.[69] In early January 1997, according to an unconfirmed February report, twelve South Korean evangelists "disappeared" near China's border with North Korea. South Korean government officials were aware of the alleged incident, but they were reportedly unwilling to use diplomatic channels to bring the incident to the attention of Chinese officials for fear of upsetting relations. Three South Korean men detained in June allegedly confessed to "setting up missionary posts, soliciting believers and looking for agents to propagate their religion in Shanghai."[70] They were subsequently expelled and their resident permits confiscated. By July 1997, at a briefing for foreign reporters, Han Wenzao, CCC president, openly condemned South Korean missionary activity and the secrecy with which it was being conducted.[71]

Legal restrictions on the education and training of religious practitioners have facilitated government crackdowns on evangelical pastors and lay instructors. The case of thirty-one-year-old Fu Xiqiu, now in the U.S., is an example.

In China, Fu, a Christian since 1989, had to lead a double life, teaching English in the elite Beijing Party School but at the same time running a Christian training center. On May 9, 1996, after the first twenty-five students had completed their required three months of training and were at least minimally prepared to work in the flourishing rural house church movement, seven men, one a Public Security Bureau officer in uniform, accosted Fu as he was leaving the Party School saying they wanted to talk with him at his home. After confiscating Bibles, video cassettes, and teaching tapes, the officers took Fu and his wife, Cai Bochun, to an interrogation center and subjected them to round-the-clock questioning. They threatened that unless the pair revealed the names of their co-workers and international contacts, their own families would be jailed. Two days after the search, husband and wife were moved to the Chongwen branch of the Beijing Police Station and asked to sign a document that accused them of illegal evangelization. Fu signed.

For the next two months both Fu and Cai were questioned intermittently. They were released on July 8, but not before signing a document admitting that they had violated two regulations, Nos. 144 and 145, and that Jonathan Chao,

---

[69] "Korean Missionaries Arrested," *China News and Church Report*, January 31, 1997.

[70] "Shanghai Expels 3 South Korean Missionaries," Agence France Presse, August 7, 1997, as reported in the Shanghai Xinmin Evening News.

[71] "China Says There's Religious Freedom," Associated Press, July 7, 1997.

president and director of China Ministries International - Chinese Church Research Center, was a Taiwanese spy and CIA operative. (Over the last few years the organization has moved its headquarters and operations from Hong Kong to Taiwan.) Police clearly expected that the couple would cooperate with them in exposing a missionary network.

On July 10, the philosophy department at People's University, where Cai had already completed all required work for her master's degree, refused to grant it. Instead she was told to report for her assigned work at the Public Transportation Company. On July 29, after repeated telephone calls about job arrangements proved unsatisfactory, Fu and Cai visited the company and were informed that Cai had to return to school. On July 13, a Mr. Ma from the Public Security Bureau picked them up, drove to a park, interrogated them about their contacts, and demanded written reports. They refused. On July 18, Fu was told that he had lost his job, that his salary was canceled, and that he had two months to move. The order, he learned, had come from "higher ups" in the Central Committee of the Beijing Communist Party and in the Beijing municipal government. By July 29, the pair had been given a few weeks to make a substantial report or face rearrest. Cai, by then pregnant, was also accused of having a baby without permission. In August, despite invitations to study in the U.S., Fu and Cai were refused clearance to travel. By September 10, knowing rearrest was imminent, they fled. By October 12, they had reached Bangkok. A co-worker also managed to escape China.[72]

Suppression of "feudal superstition"

The vast majority of worshipers in China are those whose allegiance is to what is generally termed popular religion, but they are denied recognition as adherents of a true religion.[73] Their beliefs and practices instead are relegated by the Chinese government to the realm of "feudal superstition" or "folk belief."[74]

---

[72] Human Rights Watch interview, June 1997, Hong Kong.

[73] There is no mention of popular religion in any of the campaign documents cited or in the "Regulations from the Shanghai Religious Affairs Bureau."

[74] China's new Criminal Code provides for up to seven years of imprisonment for "organizing or using secret societies or heretical religious organizations, or using superstitious beliefs to damage the implementation of state law and administrative regulation."

According to an internal party document, a major concern is the ability of superstition to enhance the influence of religion.[75] Chinese scientists, arguing the government position, maintained that "it is high time to declare war on the rising popularity of superstitious activities." They described two other major problems, both issues of government control.[76] One is the danger to social stability represented by superstitious practitioners in a position to organize complaints about local conditions; the other is their ability to arrange pilgrimages. The former strengthens the hand of those who have not benefitted from "socialist reconstruction," or who have been the target of corrupt practices, for example, those who have lost their jobs or been subject to excessive fees and taxes. Pilgrimages give people interested in changing local conditions access to ideas beyond their immediate locale. Feudal superstition, in the form of construction and maintenance of temples and tombs, or in the form of festivals and feasting, also wastes resources, including land, that would be better spent on the development of the productive forces.[77]

Differentiation of religious from superstitious belief and practice is not easy. Certain practices, such as geomancy and fortune-telling are tolerated. Others, divination, palm reading, casting of lots, exorcisms, and healing, generally are not, but censure varies from place to place. Furthermore, the rituals and beliefs of many practitioners form a syncretic blend originating in popular religion, Daoism and/or Buddhism. Association with either of the latter two removes the stigma of involvement in a non-religion. *Fazhi Ribao*, China's leading legal newspaper, did publish suggestions for an anti-superstition law that would set standards for distinguishing between superstition and legal religious customs, but to date no public information about the process is available.[78]

The campaign against superstition has led to widespread destruction of religious buildings. During a sustained campaign between February and June 1996 in the coastal province of Zhejiang, 15,000 temples, churches, and tombs were

---

[75] "Some Hot Issues."

[76] "China News and Church Update," *Tripod*, Volume XV, No. 89, p. 56, from *China Daily*, June 27, 1995.

[77] See "Funeral and Internment Reform Benefits the Nation and the People," *Renmin Ribao*, June 6, 1997, p. 4, in *FBIS*, July 1, 1997.

[78] See *China News and Church Report*, May 19, 1995.

destroyed; Ningbo, a major Zhejiang city, alone razed 3,000 temples.[79] On June 26, a provincial party committee secretary's work meeting "studied the ideas and measures for intensifying the drive..." pointing out that the work was long term and "some localities have yet to set things right...."[80] In addition to funeral and burial reform, the report promoted intense ideological education to root out "superstition and advocate science." It also affirmed the fact that the "dismantling" itself had not been completed and that some buildings, rather than being destroyed, were to be converted to other uses. Emphasis on superstition in the report is the only clue that the temples might be neither Buddhist nor Daoist.

Information from other locales or other recent incidents of suppression of popular religion had been scant, but by September 1996 the magazine *Democracy and the Legal System*, citing figures for temple restoration or construction in Fujian, Henan, and Shaanxi provinces, expressed alarm at the "resurgence of 'superstitious practices'...growing without limits in China." Part of the concern was directed at the growth of feudal practices such as "astrology, palmistry and fortune telling" outside rural communities; part at the depiction of deities in schools and cultural centers; and part at the amount of arable land occupied by tombs.[81] Seven months later, in April 1997, it was reported that the Religious Affairs Bureau and the United Front Work Department issued a joint circular ordering a strict ban on the building of temples and outdoor Buddhas. According to their figures, there are 40,000 unauthorized temples, eight times the number of legal sites, and 150 illegal Buddhas. In addition, all small temples — according to the circular they are located in rural areas — "controlled by sorcerers, witches, and professional superstitionists shall be resolutely banned."[82]

[79] Matt Forney, "God's Country,"*Far Eastern Economic Review*, June 6, 1996, p. 47.

[80] *Zhejiang Ribao*, June 27, 1996, as reported in "Zhejiang Continues Drive Against Unauthorized Temples, Churches, Tombs," BBC Monitoring Service, July 16, 1996.

[81] "Revival of Superstition," *China News and Church Report*, November 2, 1996. See also "Funeral and Interment Reform Benefits the Nation and the People," *Renmin Ribao*, June 6, 1997, in *FBIS*, July 1, 1997.

[82] "Special Dispatch: Central Authorities Decide to Take Action Against Unauthorized Temples, Statues of Buddha," *Ming Pao*, April 4, 1997, in *FBIS*, April 11, 1997.

V. REPRESSION IN XINJIANG

The rhetoric of Chinese government leaders in the Xinjiang Uighur Autonomous Region is similar to that used elsewhere. In June 1997, for example, the Xinjiang government chairman, Abdulahat Abdurixit, called on patriotic religious leaders to "energetically give publicity to the party's policy on religion, educate the broad masses of religious believers to love their country and their religions and make new contributions to the autonomous region's social stability."[83] Earlier he had reinforced the party's dictum that religion must conform to socialism.[84] But the government's efforts to control religion in Xinjiang are complicated by nascent movements for independence or autonomy, where Islam and Uighur identity are closely linked. Government assaults on unauthorized Islamic practices are difficult to separate from efforts to quell political violence, such as that which took place in the town of Yining (Ghulja in the Uighur language), Ili-Kazak prefecture, in February 1997.

The government appears to have begun an intensified campaign to bring Islam under control at a Xinjiang regional party meeting in early May 1996. The resulting document made clear that as far as Xinjiang officials were concerned, religion was an instrument for fostering separatism in the area and that both Muslims and the West were implicated in the effort.[85] A year later, Xinjiang's chairman reiterated the point, declaring that "a handful of separatists and religious elements...whipped up religious fanaticism and preached a 'holy war.' They openly

---

[83] "Xinjiang Chairman Calls on Religious Persons," *Xinjiang Ribao*, June 25, 1997, in *FBIS*, June 27, 1997.

[84] "Xinjiang Government to Crack Down on Separatists," Agence France Presse, February 8, 1997, in *FBIS*, same date. See also "Call to Resolutely Implement Party Religious Policy," *Urumqi Xinjiang Ribao*, February 25, 1997, in *FBIS*, April 18, 1997.

[85] "Xinjiang Party Branch Urges Action Against 'Unlawful Religious Activities,'" BBC Monitoring Service, May 6, 1996, from Xinjiang Television, same day. See also "Xinjiang Leader Admits Existence of Muslim Party," Agence France Presse, May 11, 1997; and "Further on Xinjiang Leader's Remarks on Muslim Party," Agence France Presse, May 11, 1997.

threatened to kill pagans..."[86] The consistent linking of separatist activity to religious "elements" by Xinjiang officials resulted in the announcement that both illegal religious activities and separatists would be the main target of law enforcement in 1997.[87] The result was a severe crackdown on religious education and publishing, mosque construction, and "illegal" religious activists and activities. Party cadres who "insist on following a religion" were also a target.[88] But details are scanty, in part due to the ban on foreign reporting from the region.[89]

Information from Ili on the religious aspect of the prefecture's rectification effort, a sustained campaign to bring all religious activities and activists under government control, comes mainly from official sources. Focusing on strengthening the management of religious affairs "according to the law," the authorities, after investigation, "shut down 105 privately-run scripture classes (*talipu*); "dispersed" 499 underground scripture students; "closed or changed to other uses" 133 mosques that had been built without approval after February 1995; "ferreted out and struck at," among others, "ringleaders of extreme religious forces"; and arrested forty illegal religious activists. In fact, the report boasted that in Ili "illegal religious activities were cleaned up...district village by village, hamlet by hamlet." Part of the work concentrated on religious activities at schools and resulted in the denial or revocation of teaching certificates to those who continued to "disseminate national separatist views." Five school officials in Nilka County No. 3 Middle School were removed.[90] The report also hints at an education

---

[86] "Latest Developments in Xinjiang -- Exclusive Interview with Xinjiang Chairman Abdulahat Abdurixit," *Hong Kong Kuang Chiao Ching*, May 16, 1997, in *FBIS*, June 10, 1997.

[87] "Xinjiang Government to Crack Down."

[88] "Xinjiang Cadres Urged to Enhance Political Discipline," Urumqi Xinjiang Television, May 23, 1996, in *FBIS*, May 31, 1996.

[89] A BBC crew that entered Yining on tourist visas on April 9 was detained on April 11 and held for ten days before being expelled to Pakistan. Officials confiscated all materials including video tapes. Crew members had managed to interview some Yining residents, and there were reports that after the expulsion, police made a "large number" of arrests ("Confiscated Materials of the BBC Crew Could Lead to More Arrests," WUNN News posting, April 29, 1997).

[90] "Ili Prefecture's Intensive Rectification Develops in Depth," *Xinjiang Ribao*, June 21, 1997, p 1, in *FBIS*, July 8, 1997.

campaign, mentioning that the prefecture has been instructing "all ethnic groups in patriotism" and had "distributed an outline on religions and laws." An unofficial report named the head of the Ghulja Islamic Society, Abdushukur Abliz, as one of those arrested. Another report noted that a forty-year-old Uighur textile worker employed at the Islamic Society was seized on March 25, but no further information about him is available.[91]

According to the National United Revolutionary Front, a Uighur nationalist group based in Kazakhstan, the crackdown was not confined to Ili.[92] In Turpan, public security officers searched 200 mosques and schools on February 16, 1997 and arrested twenty-one mullahs and other staff members from Koranic schools. Staff members who were not arrested were forced to sign pledges of non-participation in separatist activities.[93]

One aspect of the crackdown in Xinjiang has been an education campaign focused on law and regulations. The campaign was sponsored jointly by the regional United Front Work Department, the Regional Nationalities and Religious Affairs Commission, and the Xinjiang Socialist Academy and directed at "representatives from ethnic religious circles." Its purpose was to increase public awareness of the need to abide by existing laws. Another part of the campaign targeted Muslim cadres and was coupled with a harsh crackdown on illegal religious activities. The campaign was one indication that central government directives, which are often less rigorously applied in national minority areas, would be strictly enforced in Xinjiang. In May 1996, the party secretary of Xinjiang studied an allegedly successful program of "rectification" in Qiar Bage Township. Its focus was on demonstrating the advantages of party membership over religious belief. Township level party branches helped local party committees to revitalize themselves, even allocating money for a party school complete with video equipment and for building an "electronic education station." A program of agricultural, scientific, and technological training was begun in order to raise the living standards of party members as examples to the general populace of the

[91] "The Head of the Ghulje Islamic Society is Arrested," WUNN News posting, April 22, 1997.

[92] So many different reports of the February 1997 turmoil appeared from so many different sources, many of them, like the National United Liberation Front, political in orientation, that it was impossible to pin down either the scope of the unrest or numbers of arrests with any certainty.

[93] "China Said to Arrest 21 in Koranic Schools in Xinjiang," Agence France Presse, February 18, 1997, in *FBIS*, February 20, 1997.

advantages of membership. In addition, ideological education among cadres was intensified, and older cadres were pressured to renounce religion.[94] In Turpan prefecture the aim of "in-depth atheist education" was to foster tighter legal control over religion through attention to the beliefs of party members. Tactics included lectures, discussions, one-on-one "talks" and "concentrated training."

Xinjiang authorities, including the Party Propaganda Committee, the United Front Work Department, the Press and Publications Department, the Culture Department, and the Nationalities Affairs Commission, have not neglected control of religious literature. Even "formal" Islamic scriptures require approval before they may be printed; Islamic religious materials can be sold only at designated locations; and, as with all religious materials, there are strict limits on importation.[95]

---

[94] "Xinjiang Township Addresses Religion."

[95] "The Cost of Putting Business" p. 17.

VI. REPRESSION IN TIBET

Nowhere are politics and religion more intertwined than in Tibet where Tibetan Buddhism is an integral part of Tibetan national identity, the Dalai Lama is both a spiritual and political leader, and many Tibetans see political independence as the only way of ending the Dalai Lama's exile and ensuring his return. Because monasteries and nunneries are so frequently centers of support for the Dalai Lama, Chinese authorities see the control of religious institutions across the Tibet Autonomous Region (TAR) and the Tibetan areas of Gansu, Yunnan, Sichuan, and Qinghai as critical to prevent political destabilization and the spread of "splittist" sentiment. The effort at control has intensified steadily since 1994 and has been characterized by a campaign to discredit the Dalai Lama as a religious leader; a massive reeducation effort in the monasteries and nunneries to instill loyalty to Chinese rule and end support for Tibetan independence or autonomy; substitution of secular leaders for monks in the most important monasteries; and interference in the selection of the Panchen Lama, the second most important Tibetan religious figure. In the process of the campaign, now in its fourth year, more than 150 Tibetans have been arrested.

Anti-Dalai Lama campaign

The campaign to denounce the Dalai Lama was institutionalized at the Third National Forum on Work in Tibet in July 1994.[96] Two years later, it was reaffirmed in the "Outline of the Tibet Autonomous Region's Five-Year Plan for Economic and Social Development and its Long-term Target for 2010," approved on May 24, 1996 by the Fourth Session of the Sixth Regional People's Congress.[97] In a chapter on splittism, the Dalai Lama is castigated as the "chief villain," who must be "publicly expose[d] and criticise[d]...stripping away his cloak of being a 'religious leader.'" By mid-November 1996, the party chief in Tibet had launched the "final attack," blaming the Dalai Lama for "feudal superstition and for promoting a range of customs that were endangering Tibetans' ability to modernize.[98]

---

[96] For an analysis of Tibetan policy instituted at the Third Forum, see *Cutting Off the Serpent's Head: Tightening Control in Tibet, 1994-1995*, Tibet Information Network and Human Rights Watch/Asia, (New York: 1996).

[97] Published in *FBIS*, June 7, 1996, under the title "Tibet Five-Year Plan, Long Range Target."

[98] "Top Officials in Tibet Vow to Fight the Dalai Lama," Agence France Presse, November 15, 1996, in *FBIS*, same day.

Then, in mid-April 1997, the party school in Tibet announced a meeting had been held to "penetratingly expose and criticize the Dalai's crimes" through the study and publication of four articles. Its report made clear that the Party Central Committee had endorsed the assessment. One of the articles asked, in reference to the Dalai Lama, "Religious leader or obstacle to building religious order?" In it, the Tibetan leader was accused again of trying to "wreck Tibet and the Buddhist religion" and of using religion to "split the motherland."[99] The campaign has not ceased. On September 7, 1997, in the official *China Daily*, he was similarly vilified for using "the cloak of religion...to restore his previous privileges, lands and serfs...."[100]

A ban on display of Dalai Lama photographs began in November 1994 when government employees were told they could not keep his picture in their rooms. In January 1996, some temples and monasteries were ordered to remove the photos. By April the ban, initially applying only to temples and monasteries, had been published, but later in the month some public places, such as hotels, restaurants, and shops, were told they, too, would have to comply. By May 1996 schools were affected.[101] And in at least one section of Lhasa, house to house searches reportedly began on May 20.[102]

A major protest involving several hundred monks began on May 6, 1996, when a team of party cadres ordered monks at Ganden monastery, one of Tibet's most important institutions, to immediately remove all photographs of the Dalai Lama from display. When officials refused to talk with a group of monks, the latter began to sing and dance in protest and then to throw stones. One official was severely beaten in a five-minute burst of violence during the incident. The following day, a large military force which had gathered during the night, fired warning shots, then invaded Ganden. Several monks were badly hurt during the shooting; one later died of his wounds. More than ninety monks were detained, and at least fourteen were sentenced. Two days after the incident began, Ganden was closed for rectification.

---

[99] "China Gathers Support on Tibet, Opens New Phase in Anti-Dalai Lama Campaign," TIN News Update, 1 July, 1997.

[100] "Dalai Followers Strive in Vain."

[101] "Anti-Dalai Lama Campaign Shifts to Schools," TIN News Update, 20 May, 1996.

[102] "House to House Searches for Photographs Begin," TIN News Update, 21 May, 1996.

In late June 1997, there were reports that immediate enforcement of the ban had been somewhat relaxed. The head of the Religious Affairs Bureau in Tibet reportedly admitted that it "takes times to change people's mentality...It is up to us to persuade the population to stop worshiping his image."[103]

Reform and reeducation in the monasteries

Third Forum policy also set out guidelines for stricter supervision of monasteries and nunneries. As part of the effort, officials targeted the composition of Democratic Management Committees, leadership bodies that had responsibility for such items as monastic discipline and curriculum. These committees were set up in each monastery in the 1950s and reinstituted when the monasteries reopened after having been closed down during and after the Cultural Revolution (1966-76). Following the Third Forum, candidates for those leadership positions first had to be vetted by secular authorities.

The order was combined with a program to "reeducate" all monks and nuns in patriotism and to adapt the tenets and practices of Tibetan Buddhism to a socialist society. In addition, the government put a new emphasis on programs to limit both the numbers of monks and nuns and the numbers of monasteries and nunneries. In June 1995 an official team was created to register all temples and monasteries. In February 1996 Chinese leaders ordered the closure of politically active monasteries and required the replacement of all monastic leaders not certified as patriotic. Officials boasted at that time that "The overwhelming majority of lamaseries and the broad masses of monks and nuns in our region have been able to make a clean break politically with the Dalai...However, we should also soberly see that the negative influence of religion has expanded to a certain extent in recent years and that numerous problems still exist in some lamaseries." By December, according to the official *Tibet Daily,* a new "management team" was inaugurated at Drepung, the largest monastery in Lhasa, charged with running its affairs and finances and ensuring that all its monks were appropriately patriotic.[104] Speeches at the inauguration ceremony indicated that after five months of reeducation, a thorough purge of "reactionary" personnel had been completed. It is not known what happened to those who were purged.

The reeducation campaign, which began at Tibet's three most famous monasteries, Sera, Drepung, and Ganden, had reached some fifty monasteries and

[103] "China Gathers Support."

[104] December 12, 1996.

nunneries by June 1997, according to one report.[105] By September 1997, more than 900 of 1,700 monasteries had been reached, with 30,000 of 46,000 monks and nuns affected.[106] In the exact language used by Han Wenzao of the Chinese Christian Council, Tibetan officials compared the crackdown on monasteries to steps taken in the U.S. against the Branch Davidians and in Japan against the Aum Shinrikyo.[107] Ragdi, executive secretary of the Communist Party Committee of the Tibetan Autonomous Region, went so far as to say that the political indoctrination campaign and democratic management had rescued the monasteries from chaos. Reports in June, however, implied that officials had reassessed the drive because the harsh tactics and penalties employed were backfiring.[108]

As originally conceived, the campaign was designed to educate monks in patriotism and "the views of the government," "implement the party's policy of religion totally and correctly," and create "harmonious co-existence between the religious and socialist societies." It included a demand that monks express their opposition to the Dalai Lama.[109] Reeducation teams, averaging one member to four monks, lived at monasteries for three months; some teams, in a show of political clout, included senior provincial and prefectural officials.

A July 15, 1996 document issued by the Sera Democratic Management Committee, "The Important Points to be Understood by All the Sera Monks During the Study Session," is the most complete account of the drive's purposes and

---

[105] "Rural Monks Reject Patriotic Education," TIN News Update, July 31, 1997.

[106] The figures were given by Ragdi, executive secretary of the Communist Party Committee of the Tibetan Autonomous Region, at a press conference on September 17, 1997 in Beijing while the Fifteenth Party Congress was in session. See also "Tibet Officials Defend Religious Crackdown," Agence France Presse, September 17, 199 7, in FBIS, September 22, 1997; "Raidi, Wang Lequan Comment on Situation in Tibet, Xinjiang," Xinjiang Ribao," September 18, 1997, in FBIS, September 19, 1997.

[107] "Crackdown against monasteries defended," South China Morning Post, September 19, 1997.

[108] "China Gathers Support."

[109] "Re-education Campaign Extended to all Tibet Region," TIN News Update, September 7, 1996.

methods available.[110] At Sera, which housed some 400 monks, a "bad attitude" in reeducation classes was grounds for expulsion. Monks were required to study four textbooks, part of the series "Explanations and Proclamations for the Propagation of Patriotic Education in Monasteries Throughout the TAR";[111] be quiet and disciplined, stay until the end, and take notes at lectures; keep their reeducation manuals clean; attend meetings, smaller classes, and tutorials; do one continuous hour of homework a day; "actively speak out and contribute"; and "speak from their hearts to officials." At the time the seventy-member reeducation team was in residence, daily monastic debates were suspended.

In late August 1996, some Sera monks issued a four-page statement indicating their refusal to denounce the Dalai Lama and to yield to other demands of the "Loving the Motherland and Loving Religion" campaign. By this time, some thirteen monks had been arrested for activities related to their refusal to go along with the campaign.

The regulations for Drepung monks, similar to those at Sera monastery, called for each monk to speak out "one by one"; for written and oral exams; and for those monks "with bad attitudes and poor results" to be expelled. The "Five Points, Two Choices" system in place at Drepung gave monks little room for differences of opinion. Either they were willing to denounce the Dalai Lama, accept that Tibet had been a part of China for centuries, and acknowledge the legitimacy of the Chinese government's selection of the new Panchen Lama, or they could resign.[112] The case of twenty-one-year-old Ngawang Tharchin is an example. On October 25, 1996, two weeks after interrupting a lecture by a well-known Tibetan historian to deny that Tibet had been an integral part of China for centuries, he was administratively sentenced to a three-year "reeducation through labor" term which he reportedly is serving in Trisam prison. Four others were taken into custody in connection with the drive, and at least sixteen resigned before sitting for the written exam. Officials had distributed the correct answers in

---

[110] "Re-education Drive: Sera Monks Issue Statement - Arrests Climb to 13," TIN News Update, September 18, 1996.

[111] The series was put out by the Administrative Office for the Propagation of Patriotic Education in Monasteries Throughout the Tibet Autonomous Region. Each consisted of an "explanation" on respectively "Tibetan History," "Opposing Splittism," "Knowledge of the Law," and "Religious Policy."

[112] "Re-education Drive."; "Expulsions, Arrests, Death Reported During Re-education Drive," TIN News Update, November 27, 1996.

advance to ensure that the monks knew explicitly what was expected of them in written form.

Some 150 monks at Ganden monastery were formally expelled at the end of August 1996 for "going against the nation" by failing to answer some questions correctly, for example what four crimes the Dalai Lama had committed. Ninety-two of them were ordered not to go to Lhasa unless they were from there originally but to become farmers or traders outside the capital. Officials made clear that none of the ninety-two would be able to rejoin a monastery.[113]

Twenty-seven-year-old Tenchok Tenphel, a monk from Sakya monastery, some eighty kilometers outside of Lhasa, died on September 14, 1996 in the Sakya detention center, the end result of an argument with reeducation officials.[114] He had been arrested on September during a ritual dance performance in front of Chinese officials. Although his family was told he had committed suicide, local sources reported he died of abuse. His body was cremated without family members having viewed it and apparently without an autopsy being performed. A second monk, Gendun Gyaltsen, the caretaker of the main chapel, was taken away in metal thumb cuffs on August 23 after pictures and cassettes of the Dalai Lama were found in his room. Released after a week, he was expelled from the monastery.

Reports from rural areas indicate that as late as June 1997, monks were still passively refusing to cooperate with reeducation officials. In Gongkar county, Jampel Tendar, a twenty-year-old from Choede monastery, was arrested after several monks refused to denounce the Dalai Lama in writing. Instead they chanted prayers for him and argued against claims that it was actually China that had introduced religious freedom to Tibet and that had financed reconstruction of Choede. In Nyemo county monks were locked in their rooms for at least three weeks for their intransigence, and in Tsethang county, Tandruk Samdrubling monks walked out en masse on June 18 after reeducation began. Refusing to comply with instructions to denounce the Dalai Lama, they opted to close the monastery and go home. At Terdrom nunnery in the Drigung area, some fifty miles northeast of Lhasa, more than half the 240 resident nuns were expelled after reeducation ended in December 1996.[115]

---

[113] "Expulsions, Arrests."

[114] "Expulsions, Arrests."

[115] "Rural Monks Reject."

The Panchen Lama affair

On May 15, 1995, the Dalai Lama announced that a six-year-old child named Gendun Choekyi Nyima was the reincarnation of the tenth Panchen Lama who had died in 1989.[116] The Panchen Lama, second only in importance to the Dalai Lama in Tibetan Buddhism, was traditionally based at Tashilhunpo monastery in Shigatse, Tibet. Chinese government officials moved quickly to denounce the Dalai Lama's "interference" in the selection process and take control of it themselves. They arrested fifty-eight-year-old Chadrel Rinpoche, the abbot from Tashilhunpo, who had been in charge of the official search team, and some sixty other monks and laypersons who opposed the Chinese position. In due course, Chinese authorities announced the name of their choice and initiated elaborate installation ceremonies, trying through their own interpretations of history to justify secular involvement in a religious affair. The importance of the Panchen Lama issue to the Chinese government was highlighted in a 1996 internal document which argued that "by appointing a Living Buddha, it (the Dalai clique) seizes the control of a monastery...tantamount to seizing a position previously occupied by the communists."[117]

Several weeks before the Dalai Lama's announcement, Xinhua had announced the adoption of a "Detailed Rule on the Reincarnation of Living Buddhas, which according to the report would "separate political actions from religious affairs."[118] According to other sources, the intent of the regulation was to be able to enforce secular control over all reincarnations. The regulation has never been made public.

Both Gendun Choekyi Nyima, now eight years old, and Chadrel Rinpoche disappeared within days of the May 15 announcement. It took a year for any information about the boy to surface and almost two before any news about the abbot was forthcoming. The Chinese government finally acknowledged that Chadrel Rinpoche had been sentenced on April 21, 1997 to a six-year term and three years' subsequent deprivation of political rights for allegedly "conspiring to split the country," "colluding with separatist forces abroad," "seriously

---

[116] See "*Cutting Off the Serpent's Head*," pp. 4-5 and pp. 52-70.

[117] "Some Hot Issues." This is a variation on a common standard saying of party officials to mean that control of a monastery is, in fact, tantamount to control over an entire district.

[118] "Tibet Passes Rule on Religious Freedom," *Reuter*, April 29, 1995, from Xinhua, same day.

jeopardizing the national unification and unity of ethnic groups," and "leaking state secrets." Authorities did not disclose his whereabouts, and his trial was closed because "state secrets" were involved.[119]

It was not until September 9, 1997 that Human Rights in China reported that Chadrel Rinpoche was being held in poor conditions in a secret compound in Chuangdong No. 3 Prison, Dazu county, Sichuan province. Located behind an isolated "strict observation brigade" used to punish recalcitrant prisoners, the compound is forbidden to all but three people, two commissars who report directly to the Ministry of Justice and a prisoner who acts as a guard and a cook. Chadrel Rinpoche was reportedly taken there shortly after sentencing. He is reported to be denied all outside contacts and is not permitted to leave his cell. In July, Chadrel Rinpoche, already in poor health, reportedly began a hunger strike in protest.

The secrecy surrounding Chadrel Rinpoche's detention continues a pattern that began immediately after he was taken into custody in Chengdu, Sichuan province, on May 17, 1995. For the next six months, Chinese authorities refused to admit that he was detained, despite the fact that on July 11 the TAR's two top leaders, Gyaltsen Norbu, chairman of the TAR government, and Ragdi, were present when a fifteen-page report condemning him was read to assembled Tashilhunpo monks. On July 14, he was formally replaced as head of the monastery's management committee by a pro-Beijing hard-liner. On August 21, Chinese authorities reported that Chadrel Rinpoche was ill and hospitalized for treatment. An article in *Tibet Daily* on November 4 referred to unnamed people in responsible positions at Tashilhunpo who had cooperated in a "conspiracy with the Dalai clique" to undermine the Panchen Lama selection process. Chadrel Rinpoche was first referred to by name in an article in a Xinhua dispatch on November 30, which described him as a "criminal" involved in a "conspiracy." By December, the campaign to denounce him was in full swing. He was officially labeled a criminal and the "scum of Buddhism." In May 1996, the Chinese government, still trying to discredit him, removed him from his post on a regional committee.

As for Gendun Choekyi Nyima, after a year of denials, China's ambassador to the U.N. in Geneva finally admitted on May 28, 1996 that he was "put under the protection of the government at the request of his parents." He did not say where in Beijing the child was being held but claimed he was in good condition and that his parents were with him. According to Xinhua, "the boy was at risk of being kidnaped by Tibetan separatists and his security has been threatened."

---

[119] Two alleged accomplices were tried at the same time. His assistant, Champa Chung, was sentenced to a four-year term, and Samdrup, a businessman, was sentenced to two years in prison.

VII. HONG KONG

Religious communities in Hong Kong remain uncertain as to whether the Hong Kong Special Administrative Region (SAR) government will place any restrictions on their ability to operate, and there is considerable speculation about possible trade-offs that some of the communities might make. Are religious bodies, for example, willing to give up involvement in "political" issues, such as speaking out on restrictions of civil liberties, in the hope of ensuring freedom to run their own affairs? Will they be tempted to take pro-China or pro-SAR government positions in exchange for control of their day-to-day operations? It is their prerogative to do so and China's prerogative to encourage such actions. The question, unanswerable at this point but one that suggests religious freedom in Hong Kong bears watching, is whether self-censorship today will encourage or protect against violations of basic rights in the future.

Reverend Chu Yiu-ming from Chai Wan Baptist Church, a founder and executive committee member of the Hong Kong Alliance in Support of the Patriotic Democratic Movement in China, worries that self-censorship is well underway. Branded a subversive by Beijing, Reverend Chu, now in the U.S. for study, had been a leader in organizing the Alliance's work of aiding mainland dissidents and keeping alive the memory of the June 4, 1989 massacre in Beijing. For more than eight years, he has maintained close ties with the overseas dissident community. As a result of his activities and outspokenness, others in the religious community began to pressure him as early as 1990 to quit the Alliance.[120]

The 1984 Sino-British Joint Declaration and several articles of the Basic Law, the mini-constitution of the SAR, appear to ensure that religious institutions and believers will be treated the same under Chinese rule as they were under the British colonial administration. Article 32 of the Basic Law guarantees freedom of religious belief and the freedom to manifest that belief in public.[121] Article 141 guarantees that the government will not interfere in the internal affairs of religious organizations; that they will be able to maintain their property rights and run seminaries, schools, hospitals, and welfare institutions; and that they will be able

---

[120] "Troubled soul ready to go the extra mile," *South China Morning Post*, May 30, 1997, p. 19.

[121] "Hong Kong residents shall have freedom of conscience. Hong Kong residents shall have freedom of religious belief and freedom to preach and to conduct and participate in religious activities in public."

51

to extend their ties to external religious organizations and believers.[122] Articles 136 and 137 preserve the basic structure of the educational system, guarantee autonomy and academic freedom to educational institutions, permit schools run by religious organizations to provide religious education, and permit students freely to choose their educational institutions.[123]

These guarantees are weakened by a number of other provisions. Most fundamentally, the power to interpret the Basic Law rests ultimately with the National People's Congress in China, so if religious organizations want to challenge a perceived infringement of the above rights in a court of law, the final arbiter will be a body that has not shown itself to be particularly independent of the party leadership, especially in sensitive cases. Article 23 of the Basic Law is also a source of major concern to church leaders. It requires the Hong Kong legislature to enact laws "to prohibit any act of treason, secession, sedition, subversion against the Central People's Government" and "prohibit political organizations or bodies of the Region from establishing ties with foreign political organizations or bodies." Financial and other kinds of links to international religious organizations may be interpreted as ties to foreign political organizations.

---

[122] "The Government of the Hong Kong Special Administrative Region shall not restrict the freedom of religious belief, interfere in the internal affairs of religious organizations or restrict religious activities which do not contravene the laws of the Region. Religious organizations shall, in accordance with the law, enjoy the rights to acquire, use, dispose of and inherit property and the rights to receive financial assistance. Their previous property rights and interests shall be maintained and protected. Religious organizations may, according to their previous practice, continue to run seminaries and other schools, hospitals and welfare institution and to provide other social services. Religious organizations and believers in the Hong Kong Special Administrative Region may maintain and develop their relations with religious organizations and believers elsewhere."

[123] "On the basis of the previous educational system, the Government of the Hong Kong Special Administrative Region shall, on its own, formulate policies regarding the educational system and its administration, the language of education, the allocation of funds, the examinations system, the system of academic awards and the recognition of educational qualifications. Community organizations and individuals may, in accordance with law, run educational undertakings of various kinds in the Hong Kong Special Administrative Region." (Article 136)

"Educational institutions of all kinds may retain their autonomy and enjoy academic freedom. They may continue to recruit staff and use teaching materials from outside the Hong Kong Special Administrative Region. Schools run by religious organizations may continue to provide religious education, including courses in religion. Students shall enjoy freedom of choice of educational institutions and freedom to pursue their education outside the Hong Kong Special Administrative Region." (Article 137)

Some religious organizations may also fall under the purview of the Societies (Amendment) Ordinance Bill 1997 which went into effect on July 1, 1997. The ordinance exempts "religious, charitable, social or recreational" organizations from registering unless "the Societies officer gives written notice that he is of the opinion that the society is not used solely" for the purpose it claims. In addition, cancellation of registration is permissible if the Societies Officer "reasonably believes that the cancellation is necessary in the interests of national security...." Societies subject to registration may be prohibited from operating if they are affiliated with or maintain financial, managerial or policy-making ties with foreign political organizations, or if they compromise national security, public safety, public order or the rights and freedoms of others. Until such time as each of the terms in the applicable articles and ordinances is precisely defined and tested in a court of law, and until the articles and ordinances have been implemented, their impact on freedom of association and religious practice remains a subject for speculation.

Ye Xiaowen, the Religious Affairs Bureau chief, apparently tried to alleviate some of the concerns a year before the July 1, 1997 handover when he and a party of eleven, including the RAB deputy director, the deputy director of the second bureau of the United Front Work Department, and the deputy director of the RAB foreign affairs division spent ten days, June 20-29, 1996, visiting Hong Kong's religious and business leaders. At a private dinner for sixty religious leaders, Ye offered reassurances that freedom of religious belief, as guaranteed in the Basic Law, would be honored, the registration system would not be extended to Hong Kong, and religious believers would not have to support the socialist system. He added, however, that they would have to "respect the nation," "the motherland," and "not undermine Hong Kong's stability and prosperity, and love the country, Hong Kong and religion." Many noted both the order of the last part of his dictum — putting the country above religion — and that, with media banned from covering the trip, the assurances were given in private. Any future effort to hold the Chinese government to its promises would be perforce much more difficult.

Ye also addressed the issue of mainland-Hong Kong church relations, warning adherents against trying to "reform the mainland," and reiterating the guiding principle of the "three mutuals." This is a principle outlined in Article 148 of the Basic Law, which states that "the relationship between...religious organizations in the Hong Kong Special Administrative Region and their counterparts on the mainland shall be based on the principles of non-subordination, non-interference and mutual respect." Ye reminded his listeners that Regulation No.144, "Regulations on the Supervision of the Religious Activities of Foreigners in China," applied to Hong Kong residents.[124] Almost a year later, at a June 9 press conference, Ye restated Chinese policy when he declared that no RAB employee would go to Hong Kong and no Chinese religious laws or regulations were applicable to Hong Kong.[125]

Before the July 1997 reversion to Chinese rule, Chinese government initiatives left religious leaders and their constituencies the task of sorting out the political and moral implications of alternative responses to a range of issues.

The first dilemma surfaced when PRC officials became aware of the Lutheran World Federation's long-standing plans to hold its quinquennial assembly in Hong Kong within days of the handover. In essence, China threatened the Federation with cancellation and castigated the British government for not informing it of the upcoming event. British officials replied that the meeting was private and of no concern to either government. After an international outcry and extensive meetings with Lutheran organizers, Chinese authorities backed down. But the point had been made: religious activities were no longer private affairs.

Hong Kong churches and religious organizations stayed out of public protests over the affair; some observers faulted Baptist, Methodist, Anglican, Lutheran, and other religious leaders for their unwillingness to get involved. At the Lutheran assembly's close, local delegates and those from elsewhere in Asia refused to endorse a resolution about China that contained language critical of dissident treatment, administrative detention, due process shortcomings, and the death penalty, arguing that as it stood the resolution was "a great insult for the Chinese," would be "considered unfriendly," and "hurt the feelings of the Chinese people around the world." As a compromise the assembly dropped all mention of China.[126]

But if the Hong Kong religious community tried to avoid taking a stance on the Lutheran assembly, it was quick to respond to another Chinese government challenge that seemed to threaten its independence directly. A row started more than a year before the handover, when Xinhua, the official Chinese News Agency whose Hong Kong office was the *de facto* Chinese embassy there, invited churches to organize October 1, 1996 National Day celebrations. (On October 1, 1949, Mao

---

[124] Editorial, *Tripod*, Volume XVI, No. 94, p. 3-5.

[125] "Government to Guarantee Religious Freedom of HK Residents," Xinhua, June 9, 1997. in *FBIS*, June 12, 1997.

[126] "Lutheran church drops criticism of China," *South China Morning Post*, July 24, 1997.

Zedong had proclaimed the founding of the People's Republic of China, and by the time of the debate, it had already been decided that starting in 1997, October 1 would be a public holiday in Hong Kong.) Those religious figures who wanted to accept the invitation argued that church participation would prevent mainland officials from dictating the form of the Hong Kong festivities. Others argued that official church participation would open the door to the Chinese government's use of the church as a political tool. If individual churchgoers wished to participate there were sufficient opportunities to join celebrations organized by lay groups. In the end, religious organizations and individuals participated in a variety of activities, some church organized, some not. But the tactic had helped Beijing identify religious figures likely to oppose secular interference in religious affairs.

Another divisive issue emerged in the wake of the Chinese government's decision on March 24, 1996 to disband Hong Kong's elected Legislative Council (Legco) as of midnight June 30, 1997 and to replace it with an interim appointed body. The task of "electing" the provisional members, which fell to a 400-member Selection Committee whose other major responsibility was to choose the SAR Chief Executive, gave rise to a highly technical and contentious debate over the religious community's participation in the process of choosing the Selection Committee itself. Again, the division was between those who felt that participating in the Selection Committee encouraged Chinese interference in Hong Kong affairs and those who believed that religious activities would be better protected by working within pro-China institutions.

The Hong Kong Catholic Church

Hong Kong Catholic Church officials have been guarded in public assessments of their relations with China, expressing optimism, caution, and uncertainty at the same time. A diocesan news release characterized the theme of a Catholic celebration on October 20, 1996 as the Catholic Church's determination to continue to serve the local community despite anticipated difficulties.[127] On January 13, 1997, in his annual address on the state of the Catholic Church and the world, Pope John Paul II expressed concern for Hong Kong, saying that the Vatican would follow developments there with particular interest because of the "size and the vitality of the Catholic community." Bishop Zen Ze-kiun, ordained as Coadjutor Bishop of Hong Kong on December 6, 1996 and thus in line to succeed Hong Kong Cardinal Wu Cheng-chung, suggested that the Pope's remarks

---

[127] "25,000 Catholics Pray on Mission Sunday for the Future of Hong Kong," UCANEWS, October 24, 1996.

were simply a concern for the territory and not directed at Chinese authorities.[128] A week before the handover, the Pope again expressed concern for and solidarity with Hong Kong Catholics.[129]

In April 1997, Bishop Zen, referring to worries over religious controls, continued to express confidence. "Although I understand and share the feeling of common people," he said, "there are also good promises in the Joint Declaration and the Basic Law, and there are many reasons to be optimistic."[130] On the other hand, Auxiliary Bishop Tong Ho, also ordained on December 6, reminded Hong Kong Catholics that as far as their activities related to the Chinese Church were concerned, they had best remain low key.[131] And on June 17, two weeks before reversion to Chinese rule, a Vatican document voiced fears over Beijing's arbitrary legal interpretations; it denounced the restrictions on free association and expression embodied in the amended Societies Ordinance, saying, "A Christian organization which wants to talk politics risks doing something illegal if it is revealed that in its budget, there is cash aid from abroad."[132] Three days later a foreign ministry spokesman replied, "After July 1, the affairs of Hong Kong are purely a domestic matter for China."[133]

Along with their roles as major spokesmen for the Hong Kong church, Bishop Zen and Bishop Tong have been engaged in dialogue with high-level Chinese religious affairs personnel. On May 20, a little over a month before the handover, the two new bishops and the vicar-general began two days of meetings in Beijing with the head of the Religious Affairs Bureau, the deputy director of the United Front, and the deputy director of the Hong Kong and Macao Affairs Office.

---

[128] "Pope Says the Holy See is Keeping a Close Watch on Hong Kong," UCANEWS, January 16, 1997.

[129] "Hong Kong July 1 Mass Calls Catholics to Face Challenges Ahead and to Serve People," UCANEWS, July 2, 1997.

[130] "Coadjutor Bishop Says Optimism Best Strategy," UCANEWS, April 24, 1997.

[131] "Bishops-Elect Hold History-Making Dialogue with Laity," UCANEWS, November 18,1996.

[132] "Vatican Voices Fears Over Post-handover Situation," *Hong Kong Standard*, June 18, 1997, p. 2, in *FBIS*, June 19, 1997.

[133] "Spokesman Tells Vatican Not to Interfere," Agence France Presse, June 20, 1997, in *FBIS*, June 23, 1997.

They also met with Bishop Zong Huaide (now deceased), then president of both the Chinese Catholics Bishops Conference and the Catholic Patriotic Association.[134] The initiative originally came from Xinhua but was repeatedly refused until after the Hong Kong bishops' ordinations. In mid-April Hong Kong church officials approached Xinhua. An invitation from the RAB arrived on May 9.

The *Sunday Examiner,* the Hong Kong diocesan newspaper, in its lead article on June 1 characterized the secret meetings as discussions; the word negotiation appears nowhere in the article.[135] But Bishop Zen did say that "rather than rely on the media, Hong Kong church representatives should express their views directly to Beijing officials and ascertain their position on various matters concerning the Catholic Church in Hong Kong after July 1." Others have said that things have to be "spelled out whether or not the PRC wants to listen." The inference is that the "discussions" will be ongoing. A more fundamental issue is whether the affairs of the 150-year-old Hong Kong Church are in any way the concern of Beijing.

One obvious problem under discussion is the future role of the Catholic Church in educating the children of Hong Kong and in continuing to be a major provider of health and social services.[136] Ye Xiaowen in his June 1996 meeting with Catholic leaders in Hong Kong did inquire about Catholic education, but he seemed to be primarily interested in the financing of seminary education.[137] At the time of the handover, the Catholic Church ran one fifth of all Hong Kong schools, including kindergartens, elementary, middle, and upper schools, and vocational, special education, adult, and evening facilities. In return it has received tax incentives and land grants to build both churches and schools.[138] Overall enrollment

---

[134] Bishop Zong died of a heart attack on June 27, 1997.

[135] "HK Catholic leaders visit China," Volume LI, No. 22, June 1, 1997.

[136] The Hong Kong Catholic Church administers six hospitals, nine clinics, fourteen social service agencies, eleven hostels, twenty-nine old-age homes and centers for the handicapped ("Between Pessimism and Optimism," *Tripod*, Volume XVII, No. 99, p. 10).

[137] "China News and Church Updates," *Tripod*, Volume XVI, No. 94, p. 52.

[138] Mary M.Y. Yuen, "The Catholic Church in Political Transition," in Joseph Y. S. Cheng (ed), *The Other Hong Kong Report 1997*, (The Chinese University Press: Hong Kong, 1997, pp. 505-528).

in Catholic primary and secondary schools accounted for 25 percent of Hong Kong's entire student population,[139] even though only 4 percent of Hong Kong's population is Catholic.[140] At least another 25 percent of schools are run by other Christian churches or church-related organizations.[141]

Funding for church-administered education until reversion came primarily from the Hong Kong government, with wealthy patrons also contributing heavily to church coffers. According to some observers, the system resulted in a church reluctant to speak out against the colonial government and one which avoided involvement in sensitive political questions.[142] Those same church-watchers are monitoring the Catholic Church's reaction in the face of civil liberty rollbacks — it has been fairly quiet thus far. It is under no obligation, indeed, to speak out. The issue for the Church's critics is again whether silence will facilitate the Chinese government's intrusion into areas such as funding, faculty selection, and curriculum in a way that becomes restrictive of religious freedom. As of late 1997, there was no evidence of such intrusion.

The question of Catholic foreign missionaries in Hong Kong has also been raised. There is apprehension that those with only the right of abode will be asked to leave and will not be permitted to return. When asked about the status of some 400 non-Chinese priests, brothers, and nuns in Hong Kong, Bishop Zen expressed confidence that there would be no problem. "We will tell the government we need them," he said, "and if anything unjust is done to them, we have to say something."[143] But by mid-June 1997, a Vatican news service in a bluntly worded document took up the visa status of 178 missionaries, commenting that, "Everything seems to be in the arbitrary hands of Beijing...Perhaps Beijing wants to barter with the local church and exchange these permits for strictly religious activity and silence on certain social questions."[144]

---

[139] "Coadjutor Bishop Says."

[140] These figures do not include foreign workers in Hong Kong.

[141] "Christian Churches in Hong Kong Under Colonial Rule," *Tripod*, Volume XVII, No. 98, p. 29.

[142] The major exception was the Hong Kong Catholic Church's involvement in organizing the Patriotic Alliance in Support of June 4.

[143] "Coadjutor Bishop Says."

[144] "Vatican Voices Fears."

Over and above its commitment to its own constituents, the Hong Kong Catholic Church has tried to function as a bridge church, mediating between the Chinese government and the Vatican to help foster normalization of ties and between the official Chinese Catholic Church and the underground church to bring about a reconciliation. Bishop Zen Ze-kiun, at a press conference immediately following his ordination, spoke to the issue, saying he would be delighted if he could play a part in normalization.[145] In April 1997, he made explicit that the Hong Kong Catholic Church did indeed have a role in China and was performing it well. But he then made several enigmatic statements related to Sino-Vatican relations that belied his words. Sino-Vatican relations, he said, were a matter for high diplomacy — "not even bishops have access to such top secrets." His impression, he went on, was that China was not interested in pursuing dialogue since the Vatican had no business interests in China, but he hoped that agreements could be reached soon. As for the Hong Kong Church's mediation efforts, Bishop Zen made it clear that no undermining of the Catholic Church's universality could be tolerated. "We encourage Church people in China (by telling them) we are one Church," he said, "and we appreciate their loyalty to the Church despite difficult situations. We still support them, but not their abnormal position."[146] But Bishop Zen did make clear that more understanding of both the underground and official churches was necessary and neither body should be reproached.[147]

Bishop Tong privately expressed the view that the two ostensible obstacles to Sino-Vatican normalization, ties with Taiwan and authority over the appointment of bishops, were not so intractable as they might appear.[148] Publicly he has said that, in fact, the bishop issue is a major roadblock,[149] and that the Catholic Church in Hong Kong will treat members of both the official Chinese church and the underground as brothers and sisters as a means of fostering mutual understanding.[150]

---

[145] "Two New Hong Kong Bishops Hope for Solidarity with Mainland China," UCANEWS, December 12, 1996.

[146] "Coadjutor Bishop Says."

[147] "Bishops-Elect Hold."

[148] Interview, Hong Kong, June 1997.

[149] "Bishops-Elect Hold."

[150] "Two New Bishops Intent on Strengthening Relations With China Church," UCANEWS, October 28, 1996.

The issue of Chinese authorities usurping the Pope's prerogative to appoint bishops even came up in relationship to the appointment of the new Hong Kong bishops. Persistent rumors that these appointments were vetted in Beijing were categorically denied by Bishop Tong.[151] But the bishops' close relations with Chinese authorities and with Hong Kong's leaders appear to have influenced the Vatican's choices. And, despite denials, speculation has lingered that the appointments were aimed at ensuring Vatican influence in Hong Kong and preempting projected Chinese interference after July 1. At the end of November 1996, Tung Chee-hwa, then a candidate for the post of chief executive, at a meeting with Catholic representatives from the Hong Kong diocese, maintained that while the Catholic Church could continue to preserve and develop its relations with its sister churches in other countries, official ties with the Vatican were a political issue. He went on to stress that China would tolerate no foreign interference in its affairs.[152] As noted above, Regulation No. 144 on supervising foreigners' religious activities in China applies to Hong Kong-based religious organizations and personnel as well.

A reminder that the state controls religious practice in China and that religious organizations, clergy, and congregants in Hong Kong are at risk of losing their religious rights came on December 3, a few days after Tung's remarks. The Pope, in a message meant for both Chinese authorities and Chinese Catholics, asked for unity and legalization of the underground church. He asked church members to "remain loyal to the faith received and passed on" and went on to reassure Chinese authorities that a Christian could "live his faith in any political system, provided that there is respect for his right to act according to the dictates of his own conscience and his own faith."[153] A major counter-offensive ensued. Two days later, a Foreign Ministry official rejected the overture, restating the official Chinese position. "The Vatican," he said, "must stop interfering in China's

---

[151] Interview, Hong Kong, June 1997. On January 14, 1997, a spokesman for China's Ministry of Foreign Affairs hinted that the Chinese government may be "in charge" of appointing the Hong Kong bishop ("Beijing Hints That It May Appoint SAR Bishop; 250,000 Catholics in Hong Kong Will be Compelled to Sever Ties With Vatican," *Ping Kuo Jih Pao*, January 15, 1997, p. A2, in *FBIS*, January 15, 1997.)

[152] "Post-1997 Chief Executive Candidates Reassure Religious Freedom," UCANEWS, December 4, 1996.

[153] "Message of the Holy Father to the Church in China," *Tripod*, Volume XVII, No. 97, p. 32.

internal affairs, including interfering in internal religious affairs." Bishop Zong Huaide castigated the Pope for "not understand[ing] China's actual conditions," insisting that every believer enjoys a normal and happy religious life.[154] Bishop Zong went on to say that Chinese Catholics do recognize the Pope as their spiritual leader and pray for him daily. Liu Bainian, vice-chairman of the China Catholic Patriotic Association, in response to the Pope's message, reiterated the official position, that church communion is a political rather than a religious issue, that the underground church refuses to support the socialist system, and that bishops must be patriotic and act according to the country's condition.

On January 14, 1997, the Chinese Foreign Ministry spokesman in a routine press conference reiterated the Chinese government's position;[155] and at the celebration of the fortieth anniversary of the founding of the Chinese Catholic Patriotic Association, Vice Premier and Foreign Minister Qian Qichen again stressed that only after the Sino-Vatican political relationship is addressed can the religious aspects be discussed.[156]

Protestantism in Hong Kong

The Protestant clergy in Hong Kong, by and large, has been willing to confine their activities to the spiritual sphere or to go along with what China has asked of them politically, such as participation in the Selection Committee. Several incidents have fueled concern that these churches are erring on the side of caution and in the process compromising religious freedom in the SAR.

The most telling involves Deng Zhaoming, the highly respected and outspoken director of the Christian Study Centre on Chinese Religion and Culture and editor of *Bridge* magazine. Deng was asked to retire because of his pointed criticisms of political control of religion in China and his documentation of persecution of believers and of corruption within the TSPM. In a compromise he was given permission to stay until the end of 1997 rather than leave, as requested, before July 1. *Bridge* will end publication when he leaves. Its funding sources have been drying up; as one informant bluntly reported, "No one wants to be caught with *Bridge* on his shelves."

---

[154] "China Accuses Pope of Internal Meddling," *New York Times,* December 5, 1996.

[155] "Spokesman on Normalizing Relations with Vatican," *FBIS,* January 15, 1997, from Xinhua, January 14, 1997.

[156] "Chinese Catholic Patriotic Association Celebrates 40 Years," UCANEWS, September 15, 1997.

Even before he leaves officially, Deng has found himself increasingly isolated by the Hong Kong religious community. No one has disputed his facts; they have faulted him for publicizing the problems. A graduate of the Protestant Nanjing Theological Seminary, the most prestigious in China, Deng initially supported the way the Communist Party organized the religious community around the three-self principle. Years of direct exposure led to increasing disillusionment with Chinese church leaders who, he believes, violated their commitment to preserve religious freedom.

The Hong Kong-based missionary organizations also have had to rethink their options. The guidelines, if there are any, are murky at best. An example of the kind of evangelizing and training that originates in Hong Kong comes from the January 1997 issue of *Hong Kong and China Report*.[157] As reported by a Brother Wai, who signs himself as a Hong Kong Christian, a team of nine traveled to central China for four days of training with church leaders and "co-workers." On the first day, seventy people, members of seven large house church groups operating primarily in counties surrounding the training site, were in attendance. By the last evening "more than 100 co-workers turned up." As the training emphasized establishing missions, at its completion seventeen of the trainees were sent out to neighboring provinces to "plant" churches. According to Brother Wai, "They were all given a one-way ticket to their destinations — they could only return after they have planted a church!"

Such proselytizing, as the Hong Kong contingent and the trainees were well aware, is proscribed in China even if the trainees had been members of legal registered churches. Both groups circumvented the requirements in Regulation No. 144 which limit contact between foreigners and Chinese nationals, and the three-fix policy which limits a church leader to a fixed geographic sphere. The mission account obliquely acknowledged the violations. "The village house had a closed-in yard," it read. "Once we got there we stayed inside and did not dare venture outside until after dark, for fear of detection by the police."

In fact, on July 7, 1997, less than a week after Hong Kong's reversion, the leaders of the two official Chinese Protestant organizations reiterated the policy on missionaries, acknowledging that foreign — and for purposes of religious proselytizing Hong Kong residents are foreigners — theologians and preachers were welcome in China, but the ban on foreign missionaries was correct. As Luo Guanzong, TSPM chairman, put it, "Christianity should be administered by Chinese themselves."[158]

---

[157] An unpaged publication of the Revival Christian Church: see "God Uses Ordinary People!"

[158] "China Says There's Religious Freedom."

Missionary organizations in Hong Kong are well aware that Article 23 not only could shut them down but could leave them open to prosecution. Furthermore, they recognize that with China's criminal code replacing crimes of counterrevolution with crimes of "endangering state security" Chinese authorities have a potent weapon to use against those in China who respond favorably to Hong Kong missionary efforts.

Some organizations have left Hong Kong for Singapore or Taiwan. Chinese regulations pertinent to the operation of foreign missionaries on Chinese soil will continue to apply to these groups no matter where they base their operations. However, those organizations that proselytize from Hong Kong face an additional problem. By applying the Basic Law's principle of mutual non-interference between religious organizations in the SAR and their mainland counterparts, all SAR operations, including publishing and broadcasting, could be closed down completely. Other organizations have chosen to remain but have made certain that their missionary activities are legally separate from any activities that apply only to Hong Kong. They have taken pains to comply with all SAR regulations, for example, fire, safety, and occupancy laws. Still others have opted to move closer to the official church, reasoning that the growth in the number of Christians, even if their activities are circumscribed, is better than no growth at all. Several missionary organizations now focus on social welfare work in, for example, orphanages, hospitals, clinics, and old-age homes. Finally, those Protestant missionary organizations that plan to continue to evangelize on the mainland have rethought their organizational strategies, and, perhaps most importantly, some have chosen to emulate the Hong Kong Catholic Church's "basic Christian communities" by positioning themselves to operate as decentralized cells.

VIII. CONCLUSION

There is no question that the kind of state control that China exercises over religious activities is a violation of freedom of religion. It also appears to be the case, however, that the worst forms of persecution -- lengthy imprisonment and physical abuse — have declined as the campaign to contain religion "according to law" has been stepped up. Laws on registration of religious sites have been more systematically enforced, and laws governing assembly and demonstrations, urban construction and land codes, printing and publishing, and registration and administration of social organizations have been used to control religious activities.

Officially recognized temples, churches, and mosques in many parts of China are filled to capacity. Christian and Catholics form long lines to participate in the next mass or service. The increase in the number of Buddhists worshiping at official sites has been dramatic. Members of these congregations explain that if this is the best they can get in the way of organized religion, they would rather worship this way than not worship at all; they are certainly no less devout than those who refuse to register and thus become participants in "illegal" religious activities. Officials prefer to see the crowds at authorized sites as evidence of an enlightened religious policy.[159] Certainly they recognize that for the time being, tolerating the religious devotion of its citizens may be the only way to maintain their allegiance and harness them to the cause of "socialist development." But as long as the Chinese government, fearing that religion will be used as a tool for subversion and destabilization, continues to define "legitimate" and "illegitimate" organizations in terms of willingness to accept state control, religious persecution will continue to be a fact of life for Chinese of all faiths.

---

[159] One example comes from Beijing where thirty-six of 300 Protestant meeting places have been registered and 188 are under consideration ("Over 100 Religious Establishments Reopened...").

APPENDIX I: SOME HOT ISSUES IN OUR WORK ON RELIGION

Luo Shuze

(Internal document published under the auspices of the theoretical journal of the Chinese Communist Party, Qiushi, *5, 1996)*

At the present time, the situation in our work on religion is good. At a time when ethnic and religious conflicts are erupting all over the world, even leading to frequent wars in certain countries and regions, China has successfully implemented the party's policy toward religion. Our work on religion has developed smoothly. Mutual respect and cordial coexistence prevail among the different nationalities and religions. At the same time, we need to recognize that there are problems in religion, and some of these are quite serious.

I. We must be vigilant against hostile international forces using religion in trying to "Westernize" and "divide" our country.

As we open our doors wider and wider to the outside world, hostile foreign forces inevitably intensify their efforts to infiltrate China. They use religious infiltration as the breakthrough point in their attempt to "Westernize" and "divide" China, trying to turn the question of religious belief into a political one in order to achieve pluralistic political beliefs through pluralistic religious beliefs. Since the '80s, one of their strategies for subverting the socialist countries has been the cultivation of religious forces in those countries and the use of religion as their tie with the underground political forces. In their research reports, the American Buddhist Strategic Research Institute [*meiguo fojiao celue yanjiusuo*] and Johns Hopkins School of [Advanced] International Studies suggested that the United States should use religion as a "choice weapon" for subverting China. They openly support and foster forces outside of China bent on dividing the nation, helping them establish reactionary organizations that conduct brazen propaganda to divide the country. Within our country, they support underground religious forces in establishing illegal organizations, trying to wrest leadership of the Buddhist and Daoist temples and Christian churches from the patriotic religious organizations. For example, in recent years, the Vatican in Rome secretly ordained bishops in China, and through them mustered a group of backbone elements. As a result, the underground Catholic forces have again gained ground. Another example has been the Dalai clique, which, acting on its own, appointed a Living Buddha in our country. Its tactic is that by appointing a Living Buddha, it seizes the control of a monastery. It is tantamount to seizing a position previously occupied by the communists. Supported and instigated by hostile foreign forces, illegal religious organizations in certain places in our country, in the name of religion, engage in activities designed to divide the nationalities. They have intensified such activities to the point of stirring up trouble openly in defiance of the government, vainly trying to achieve the objectives of undermining national unity, subverting the socialist system, and splitting the great motherland. In view of all this, we must maintain a high degree of political consciousness in our work on religion. Comrade Jiang Zemin pointed out at the Conference on United Front Work last year that: "Only by maintaining vigilance in time of peace and a political sense can we remain clear headed, far sighted, without losing our bearing in our daily routine when we have to attend to a thousand and one things." In handling religious problems, we must maintain a high degree of political sensitivity. We need to recognize that contradictions in religion are for the most part contradictions among the people. But the religious question is influenced to a certain extent by the class struggle and various complex international factors. Under certain conditions, contradictions among the people can turn into antagonistic contradictions, and antagonistic and non-antagonistic contradictions are often intertwined. We need to learn from the lessons of the disintegration of the Soviet Union and the precipitous changes in Eastern Europe. One of these lessons is the lowering of vigilance against Western infiltration by the use of religion. As a result of the errors of the former socialist countries in the Soviet Union and Eastern Europe in their handling of the religious question, religion became an instrument in the hands of the political dissidents for stirring up trouble when the domestic politics and economy became mired in trouble and all kinds of social contradictions sharpened. That hastened the downfall of the Soviet and East European communist parties.

II. Forces of the various cults must be firmly banned.

In recent years, certain reactionary and illegal organizations, under the signboard of religion, ran rampant, endangering social stability in some areas. Examples are the *Huhan Pai,* the "Cry Out Faction" and the *Mentuhui,* the "Disciples." Some of these organizations were set up by lawless domestic elements; others were infiltrated from outside; still others were infiltrated from outside, and then changed drastically. Incomplete statistics show that cult activities have spread to most of our provinces, autonomous regions, municipalities directly under the central government, and brought some 500,000 people under their deceptive influence. They incite people to subvert the government, rave about "fostering powerful centrifugal forces in the broad countryside where the Chinese communists find it most difficult to control," "fighting the party and government to the bitter end," and "putting the communists on trial." Some raised the slogan "seize church power first and then take over political power." They threaten the grassroots political power. Some leading elements of the cult organizations intervene in the executive, the judiciary and educational work, even taking over the role of the grassroots government. Some leading elements tyrannize the countryside, act like overlords, ride roughshod over those villagers who refuse to believe in the cults and would not take part in cult activities. They sabotage the villagers' production and livelihood, and spread rumors and heresy, taking advantage of the wishes of the villagers for "good fortune" and "peace." They created social panic, resulting in the villagers giving up productive activities in order to take part in cult activities, thus seriously disrupting normal production and life. They seriously undermine social order, practicing "faith healing," "healing by scaring away ghosts" so that the deceived villagers do not seek help from physicians when they fall ill. Some died because of the delay in seeking medical care. Some were even tortured to death. Some cult leaders instigate the villagers to attack grassroots party and government organs, even engaging in beating, smashing and looting. We must, therefore, deal with the cults severely, ban and outlaw them.

III. Firmly guide religion in such a way as to make it well adapted to the socialist society.

In the forty years and more since the founding of the New China, our party has succeeded in causing religion gradually to adjust itself to fit in with the needs of the socialist society. However, some people have raised the question: Since Marxism as the dominant social ideology advocates atheism, whereas religion stands for theism, how can one fit in with the need of the other? Using incompatibility as an excuse, certain feudal religious institutions that had long been abolished such as the hereditary system of religious leadership has been restored in certain places. It is therefore necessary emphatically to raise the question again. By religion adapting itself to the socialist society, we mean that with the establishment of the socialist society, religion must adjust itself with corresponding changes in theology, conception, and organization. We require religious believers politically to love the motherland, support the leadership of the Chinese Communist Party, adhere to the socialist path, and act within the constitution and laws of the land. At the present time, we must pay attention to consolidating the victories achieved in the reform of the religious system and the patriotic campaign against imperialism. Restoration of the abolished feudal religious privileges and the system of oppression must not be allowed. We must resolutely and effectively run the Christian churches according to the "three self" principle. It is necessary, through the patriotic religious groups and personages, to expound and interpret the religious doctrine and canon in such a way as to be in the interests of socialism; and inspire and guide the religious believers gradually to modify their negative ways detrimental to national development and social progress.

IV. Integrate the implementation of the party's policy of freedom of religious belief with the strengthening of the management of religion according to law.

Some are of the opinion that our emphasis on the management of religion according to law runs counter to the party's policy of freedom of religious belief, as if the implementation of the policy of freedom of religious belief means we should turn a blind eye to all religious activities, even to the point of letting illegal activities in the name of religion go unchecked. This view is altogether one-sided and erroneous. A basic character of a modern state is that it manages social affairs according to law, and religious affairs are no exception. In fact the implementation of the party's policy of freedom of religious belief implies the management of religion according to law. This is because, in our country, every citizen enjoys the freedom to believe or not to believe in religion. They are politically equal whether they believe in religion or not. They enjoy the same rights and have the same obligations under the constitution. A citizen exercising his right to freedom of religious belief must also fulfill his obligations. No one is allowed to use religion to oppose the party and the socialist system, undermine the unification of the country, social stability and national unity, or infringe on the legitimate interests of the state, the society, the collectives, or other citizens. No one is allowed to use religion to intervene in the state's administration, judiciary, school and public education. Therefore, comprehensive and correct implementation of the party's policy of freedom of religious belief itself implies the management of religion according to law. Religious organizations, Buddhist and Daoist temples and Christian churches are social organizations, and the practice of religion is a social activity, and as such, must subject themselves to government management and supervision.

V. Strengthen the ideological and political education of religious personages.

There are close to 300,000 clergymen and women among some 100 million religious believers in our country. How they behave has a direct and important bearing on the religious believers in terms of their spiritual and social life as well as on the political leanings of the various religions. Especially in view of the fact that between eighty and ninety percent of the believers live in the rural areas and are by and large poorly educated, their understanding of the law and religious sense are both rather primitive, and they are liable to be used by people with ulterior motives. We therefore urgently need to have a large number of clergymen and women who are politically conscious and well versed in theology, and through them, to unite with, educate and guide the believers. The overwhelming majority of the representative personages from the religious circles have for dozens of years shown utter devotion to the party and worked together with us. They love their country and their religions. They have demonstrated their worth. However, in recent years, we have paid greater attention to making political arrangements for them than their ideological education. We need to attach importance to the fact that some religious personages have shown ideological retrogression. For example, some of them collude with the splittist Dalai clique to undermine the unification of our motherland. Others revive a sense of feudal religious privileges and willfully trample on the dignity of the law, infringing on the interests of the people and undermining social stability. Although these are acts of a few individuals, they nevertheless damage our cause and constitute bitter lessons. We will pay a price if we pay attention only to making political arrangements for them and neglect necessary criticism and education. That attitude does not help them in their sound development either. It is, therefore, not only necessary to show solicitude to them politically, but also to educate them persistently and patiently in upholding the dignity of law, safeguarding the people's interests, defending national unity and the unification of our motherland, as well as upholding the principle of running the churches independently by themselves. This work must be done on a regular basis, so as to make the religious personages work hard to adapt themselves to the needs of modern social development, and consciously make contributions to bringing the religions in line with the socialist society.

VI. Enhance the sensibility of the leadership at various levels to the religious problem.

At the present time, a considerable portion of our leading cadres at various levels are not well versed in our party's basic doctrine and policy toward religion. The lower the level, the more confused is the mind of our cadres about religion. Some cadres cannot even tell religion from feudal superstition, or folk belief, not to say differentiate and correctly handle the relevant problems. They shirk from their duty to manage religion, do nothing and procrastinate, so that problems cannot be nipped in the bud. Some take a laissez-faire attitude, declaring that since there is freedom of religious belief, let everything be free. The result has been abnormal development of religion in certain places with the number of believers soaring. If this state of affairs is allowed to continue, it will inevitably result in an explosive growth of religious forces. Some even raised the erroneous slogan: "Religion sets the stage for the economy to perform." They support the development of religion with their executive power, spending large sums on the construction of temples and religious statues, artificially enhancing the influence of religion.

VII. Strengthen education in the Marxist view of religion and propagate atheism.

On his inspection tour of Sichuan, Comrade Jiang Zemin pointed out the need to minimize the influence of religion, and energetically to propagate the Marxist view of religion. This issue is of the utmost importance. In recent years, our work in this area has been rather weak. There have been few weighty articles on Marxist theory of religion and atheism. On the other hand, the religious culture has produced a fairly strong shock wave."Christmas" activities and "Christmas" cards have been pretty hot. In certain places, there emerged so-called "Study Groups of the *Book of Changes* of Zhou Dynasty," which in effect are organizations engaged in fortune telling and feudal superstitious activities. In some places, *qigong*, a system of breathing exercises, and bogus science have integrated themselves with the Tibetan sect of Buddhism. What they do is actually propagating superstition to enhance the influence of religion. Some of the active planners of these activities are actually leading cadres who have retired from their party or government jobs. So the harmful influence is all the greater. Some cadres have a muddled understanding of religion. They claim that to believe in religion is to behave oneself and refrain from doing evil things, and what's so bad about that? In addition, they assert that religion is part of the superior cultural heritage. In some cases, the enterprises incurred losses, instead of improving their management, the managerial cadres led their employees in burning incense and prostrating themselves before the image of Buddha. All this shows that the mind of certain cadres is confused. It also shows the importance of education in the Marxist view of religion and of propagating atheism.

VIII. Firmly curb and forcefully combat publications that hurt our national and religious feeling.

Such books and articles have appeared in recent years, such as *Religious Experience, Sex Customs, A Drastic Turn of the Mind*, etc. At the beginning and end of last year, there were incidents such as *Talking About the Culture of the Pig in the Year of the Pig*, and the *Exotic Sex Custom,* which seriously hurt some people's national and religious feeling, and caused incidents. In some cases, extremely undesirable results were produced even though there was no incident. Comrade Jiang Zemin has repeatedly pointed out that no national or religious matter is trifling, and the media must be extremely careful, extremely strict and extremely considerate about the relevant publications. Illegal publications must firmly be eradicated. Once they are discovered, they must be severely dealt with. At the same time, those publications that stir up religious fanaticism and extreme national sentiments must be resolutely banned.

Municom Office (1997) No. 19

Office of the CP Municipal Committee Office of the Municipal Government Forward to: the Municipal Public Security Bureau; United Front Work Department of the Municipal CP Committee.

Circular on the Opinion Concerning Carrying Out the Special Struggle to Curb the Illegal Activities of Catholic and Protestant Christians According to Law

Party Committees and Governments of the Villages and Townships, Departments of the various Municipal Organs, Factories and Mines Directly under the Municipal Authorities:

The Opinion Concerning Carrying Out the Special Struggle to Curb the Illegal Activities of Catholic and Protestant Christians According to Law drafted by the Municipal Public Security Bureau and the United Front Work Department of the Municipal CP Committee has been approved by the Municipal CP Committee and the Municipal Government. We are hereby forwarding it to you. Please seriously organize its implementation in the light of your local conditions and those of your units.

In order to strengthen the leadership of the special struggle to curb the illegal activities, the Municipal CP Committee and the Municipal Government have decided to set up a leadership team to coordinate the special struggle to curb the illegal activities of the Catholic and Protestant Christians according to law. A list of members of that leadership team follows:

Team leader: Yuan Kun

Deputy team leader: Lan Xinya

Members: Su Renjie, Wang Pinhao, Fu Linlin, Sun Xiaodong, Wu Xueming, Shen Quansong, Xu Jinrong, Chen Xiaoying, Jin Xijiang, Lu Zhenbing, Zhou Hongxia

The office of the leadership team is located in the Municipal Public Security Bureau. Su Renjie and Wang Pinhao concurrently serve as director and deputy director of the office.

71

(Official seals of the Offices of the Tongxiang Municipal CP Committee and the Tongxiang Municipal Government.)

Theme: Curbing illegal religious activities circular

To: Organizations at the village and township levels
Copies for the Municipal People's Congress, the Political Consultative Conference, the Commission for Inspecting Discipline, People's Armed Forces Department, People's Procuratorate, and the Courts.

No. of copies printed: 240

Office of the Tongxiang Municipal Committee of the Chinese Communist Party
Printed and Issued on March 1, 1997
Proof reader: Chen Jiangang   Typist: Wu Ying

SECRET   **Tongxiang Municipal Public Security Bureau**

**United Front Work Department of the Tongxiang Municipal Committee
of the Chinese Communist Party: TongPub Ye (1997) No. 41**

**Opinion Concerning Carrying Out the Special Struggle
to Curb the Illegal Activities of Catholic and Protestant Christians
According to Law**

Municipal Committee, Municipal Government:
        In recent years, under the correct leadership of the Municipal
Committee and the Municipal Government, the Party's policy toward religion
has been further conscientiously implemented, and our municipality's
management of religious affairs has embarked on the course of working within
the legal framework. As far as religion is concerned, the situation is stable on
the whole. But there are also some problems that call for our attention. Taking
the situation as a whole, infiltration and subversive activities on the part of
outside hostile forces that use religion as a means to "westernize" and "divide"
our country have increased. They are energetically fostering anti-government
forces in an attempt to "gospelize" China, trying vainly to bring about in China
the kind of evolution that is taking place in Eastern Europe and the former
Soviet Union. In our country, underground Catholic and Protestant forces are
echoing each other at a distance and establishing contacts, opposing the
government and patriotic religious organizations. Illegal Protestant activities
have been noticeable in our municipality. Some self-styled missionaries are
stirring up believers to attack the "three-self" patriotic organizations, oppose
government leadership, and obstruct the implementation of government decrees.
They have under their control or influence close to 1,000 Christian believers in
our municipality. The followers are urged not to go to "three-self"
(organizations), and taught to distinguish between "believing in God" or
"believing in the (secular) world." The self-styled missionaries talk about "no
salvation and hell after death for those who believe in "three-self." The major
problems are so-called "three struggles," "three churches," and "sixteen sites."
The "three struggles" means struggle against materialism to win over new
followers by such illegal methods as making house calls and visiting the
hospitals; struggle against the "three-self" patriotic organizations for influence,
by illegally setting up meeting places close to the open churches; and struggle
among the different religions and denominations, such as between Christianity
and Buddhism, and between the Chinese Christian Church and the True Jesus

Church. The "three churches" refer to the Christian churches in Tongxiang and
Shimen, which oppose the "three-self" patriotic organizations and government
leadership, and the Christian church in Wutong, which wants to join the "three-
self" organization, but opposes government leadership. And the "sixteen sites"
refer to the sixteen illegally established assembly sites for Christian believers:
Lutou, (illegible), Qianlin, Qitang, Shiqiao, Minxin, Puyuan, etc. These illegal
activities have already interfered with the orderly conduct of the normal
religious activities and adversely affected the building of socialist spiritual
civilization and social stability in certain areas. In our municipality, there are
446 Catholics living in eight fishing villages: South of Wutong, Wuzhen,
Puyuan, Shimen, Tudian, Hushao, Yongxiu, and Lutou. As there is only one
site for Catholic activities in Puyuan, most of the other activities are conducted
in private homes or in the Catholic churches in Jiaxing, Changan, Xiashi,
Shuanglin, and Nanxun, where believers were originally baptized. There are
also problems like minors and party members becoming religious believers and
a few fanatics who oppose the patriotic religious organizations. It is necessary
to strengthen daily management/supervision of religious activities and pay
attention to the focus of the present special struggle to curb illegal religious
activities.

In accordance with the demands put forward in the circular "On the
Opinion Concerning Carrying Out the Special Struggle to Curb the Illegal
Activities of Catholic and Protestant Christians According to Law" forwarded to
the Provincial Public Security Bureau and the Provincial Commission on
Nationalities and Religious Affairs by the Offices of the Provincial Committee
of the Chinese Communist Party and the Provincial Government, we must carry
out the special struggle to curb the illegal activities of the Catholic and
Protestant Christians according to law during the first half of this year. We
hereby report as follows our opinion on how to specifically carry out that
struggle:

I. Fundamental Task:

Resolutely outlaw the illegal meeting places (*tang*) and sites (*dian*,
literally "points") that have a background of outside infiltration, or that engage
in illegal activities, or are under the control of underground missionaries; divide
and disintegrate the underground Christian forces; crack down on the criminal
activities carried out in the name of religion that violate the law; curb the
activities of the three churches in Tongxiang, Shimen and Wutong according to
law. Divide and isolate a handful of self-styled missionaries who are opposed to
"three self"; integrate the "three churches" into the "three-self" patriotic

organization; strengthen the management of religious affairs; push ahead with the registration of sites of religious activities; disseminate in an in-depth way the Party's policy toward religion and the country's laws and regulations; turn around the opinion of some religious believers misled by a handful of anti-three-self forces; and rally the religious followers around the Party and the Government. Educate the broad masses in sound, civilized and progressive ideas and morals, so as to promote social stability.

II. Steps to be taken:

In order to strengthen the leadership of the special struggle to curb the illegal activities of the Catholic and Protestant Christians, we propose that a leadership team be set up with the Municipal Committee of the Communist Party leadership as the team leader, and the participation of responsible members of the various departments: public security, united front, religion, propaganda, the procuratorate, the courts, justice, civil affairs, education, city construction, trade union, youth and women. The team will be responsible to lead, coordinate, supervise and inspect the results of the various measures to be taken. Two subordinate offices will be established, one in charge of outlawing the illegal assembly sites, and the other in charge of handling the "three churches." Work teams to curb illegal religious activities will be established in the townships of Wutong, Shimen, Wuzhen, Lutou, Shiqiao, Minxing, Qitang and Puyuan. They will be responsible for actually implementing the various measures curbing the illegal religious activities.

According to the overall plan of our province, the current special struggle "to curb illegal religious activities, shall proceed in three stages.

The first stage: the preparatory stage

Beginning today until end of February, full preparations should be made for carrying out the special struggle. The public security organs and departments overseeing religion should concentrate their efforts and make an in-depth investigation of the illegal activities of the Catholic and Protestant Christians in their respective areas, and have a clear idea of the current situation in the Catholic and Protestant faiths, infiltration by outside forces, illegal activities and the sites of illegal Protestant faiths, infiltration by outside forces, illegal activities and the sites of illegal activities under the control of underground bishops, priests and self-styled Protestant Christian missionaries, as well as those sites that were denied registration or refused to register in 1996. Legally valid evidence should be collected and sorted out. And on that basis, work plans should be mapped out in the light of local conditions, and meetings of leadership teams convened to determine the responsibilities, tasks and measures to be taken by the various departments and standards to be met.

The second stage: the stage for action
From March to May. Concentrate all efforts and working according to an overall plan, actions should be taken in there steps:
First, work to mobilize and win over the believers through the patriotic religious organizations. The united front, religion and propaganda departments should call on and mobilize the "three-self patriotic movement committees" and Christian associations to use the forum of their open churches to propagate the Party's policy toward religion and the country's laws and regulations, educate the broad masses of religious believers to observe the regulations governing the sites of worship, and persuade these who worship at illegal sites to go and worship in the open ones, and make them see the line of demarcation between normal and legitimate religious activities on the one hand and illegal activities on the other, so as to divide and disintegrate the illegal sites of worship.
Second, ban the illegal sites of worship according to law, resolutely curb illegal religious activities, and crack down on criminal activities that violate the law (April). Large-scale illegal meetings of Catholic and Protestant Christians, illegal Protestant organizations, illegal training classes, propaganda materials illegally published, printed and distributed, and illegal assembly sites that have a background of outside (foreign) infiltration, that engage in illegal activities and are under the control by underground missionaries must be firmly curbed and banned in accordance with the country's "Law on Assembly and Demonstration," "Regulations Governing Sites of Religious Activities" and laws governing printing and publishing. The municipal people's governments should establish "education classes" to assemble, educate and reform the conveners of illegal assemblies and self-styled missionaries. They should be ordered to cease and desist form illegal activities. The illegal assembly sites established without approval should be disposed of according to law and put under long-term control of the local police stations and public security committees. Evidence should be collected of the criminal activities perpetrated in the name of religion and punished according to law.
Third, comprehensive in-depth control. The Christian churches in Tongxiang, Shimen and Wutong, which refused to register and rejected supervision after repeated persuasions, must be curbed (May). First, the departments overseeing religion should ask the "three-self" patriotic organizations and personnel to temporarily take over those churches, approve the re-establishment of Wutong (Commercial Bridge) and Shimen churches,

declare that the Wutong Baziqiao Church will not be registered, will not be protected by law and ordered to cease activities. Those churches built illegally in violation of the regulations shall be closed down temporarily in accordance with the urban construction and land control codes. Those few self-styled missionaries and conveners of the Tongxiang, Shimen and Wutong churches who refuse to observe regulations and obstruct the implementation of government decrees should be educated and controlled by relevant units under the supervision of the departments concerned. Their attempts to stir up trouble should be strictly prevented. In curbing illegal activities according to law, attention should be focused on educating, uniting with and winning over the broad masses of believers who worship at the Tongxiang, Shimen and Wutong churches. The religion and propaganda departments should energetically conduct education and propaganda work among these believers by using all kinds of methods, so that the believers will understand the line of demarcation between normal and illegal religious activities, enhance their willingness to refrain form illegal religious activities, and become patriotic, party-loving and law-abiding citizens, good believers. Work teams should be sent out work hard, relying fully on grassroots-level party and government organizations, start by guiding the masses in developing the economy to achieve a well-to-do standard of living. These efforts should be made in coordination with the building of spiritual civilization, to propagate the Party's policy and laws of the country in a widespread and profound way, so as to shake off and weaken the influences of the illegal religious activities.

The third stage: June

The stage of summing up and inspection of results to be approved by the municipal and regional authorities. The standards of approval: (1) underground Catholic and Protestant Christian forces have been divided; the overwhelming majority of the religious believers have been educated, united with and won over to take the road of loving one's country and loving the church; (2) illegal activities have in the main been halted, and criminals who have violated the law have been punished according to law; (3) illegal religious organizations have been destroyed, and the illegal assembly sites with background of foreign infiltration and under the control of underground missionaries have been banned; (4) the underground Catholic bishops, priests and self-styled Protestant missionaries who cannot yet be punished according to law, have been placed under strict surveillance; (5) the grassroots level Party and government organizations have strengthened their supervision of religious activities, with specified personnel in charge. Those in charge overseeing religious activities have a good knowledge of the situation in local religious affairs, a fair knowledge of religion, and a fair grasp of the party's policy toward religion and the relevant laws. They should be bold enough to supervise religious activities, good and resourceful at their job.

III. The standards demanded:

The various local authorities should regard the special struggle to curb illegal Catholic and Protestant Christian activities as a specific measure for carrying out the spirit of the Party's Sixth Plenary Session of the Fourteenth Congress and the Eighth Plenary Session of the Ninth Provincial Committee. It should be seriously and successfully carried out in conjunction with the current educational campaign about the Party's basic line for the rural areas launched in our province. The importance and complexity of this struggle should be fully understood. The Party's policy toward religion and the relevant laws and regulations must be strictly adhered to. Two different types of contradictions must be differentiated and handled properly, so as to ensure the successful conduct of the special struggle. In carrying out this special struggle, the various local authorities must master the following points:

(1) Work hard to investigate and collect evidence, rely fully on the laws and regulations, crack down and curbs must proceed accurately and forcefully according to law.

(2) Curbing illegal religious activities according to law must not involve sites and assembly point of normal religious activities. Those sites to be strictly supervised and temporarily denied registration should not be banned for the time being. While dealing with the three churches in Tongxiang, Shimen and Wutong under the control of the self-styled underground missionaries, conditions should be created to enable chosen patriotic missionaries to form church committees there to conduct worship activities and occupy those religious positions.

(3) Strengthen information work. As a matter of fact, those who control the Tongxiang and Shimen churches and engage in illegal religious activities are the same self-styled missionaries who compete with "three-self" for influence and illegally established thirteen assembly sites. Every move made by these backbone elements who engage in illegal activities must be placed under strict surveillance. They must be prevented form stirring up trouble. Any sign of trouble must be promptly and firmly dealt with under the unified leadership of the Party Committee and the government. Troubles must be nipped in the bud.

(4) Bring the initiative of the patriotic religious organizations into play. Educate and encourage the patriotic clergy to assist the special struggle, so that they would on their own help the government educate, unite with and win over the masses of religious believers in terms of religious feeling and consciousness.

(5) In carrying out the special struggle, the various villages and townships and departments should closely coordinate their efforts, strengthen their contacts, exchange information and work together.

(6) The news media should not publicly report on the special struggle.

Please forward the above opinion to the various local authorities and departments for implementation, if it is not found inappropriate.

Tongxiang Municipal Public Security Bureau
The United Front Work Department of the Tongxiang Municipal Committee of the Chinese Communist Party
February 27, 1997

APPENDIX III: DOCUMENT OF THE DONGLAI TOWNSHIP COMMITTEE OF THE CHINESE COMMUNIST PARTY

Dong Party Issue No. 42 (1996)

The Chongren County Committee of the Fuzhou District

The Donglai Township Committee of CPC

Circular on Transmitting the Enforcement Plan for Curbing the Illegal Activities of the Underground Catholic Church According to Law

Prepared by the Donglai Township Leadership Group for Curbing the Illegal Activities of the Underground Catholic Church According to Law

To: Village Party Branches, Units Directly Under the Township Administration

Having studied and approved the "Enforcement Plan for Curbing the Illegal Activities of the Underground Catholic Church According to Law" drawn up by the Donglai Township, we are transmitting it to you. Please conscientiously enforce it in the light of your actual conditions.

In recent years, the population of religious believers in our township has increased due to intensified infiltration by hostile religious forces and elements outside our borders and unlawful activities of underground religious forces within our country. Some have used religion to engage in criminal activities in violation of the law, seriously disturbing the social order and affecting political stability. Therefore, organizations throughout this township at every level must fully recognize the seriousness and harmfulness of the problem in an overall political sense, conscientiously strengthen the leadership, firmly and decisively organize forces to carry out this special struggle to curb the illegal activities of the underground Catholic Church according to law.

Curbing the illegal activities of the underground Catholic Church is a decisive and critical political work. In developing this special struggle, we must seek truth from the facts, and abide by the law, differentiate between the two different types of contradictions, be highly vigilant against the hostile forces and elements inciting the believers and stirring up trouble, assure the successful development of the work to "curb illegal activities." Work plans and sensitive and important problems must be promptly reported for instructions.

November 20, 1996

Subject: Circular on The Administration of Religious Affairs (and) The Struggle
to Curb Illegal Activities   Enforcement Plan

Copies for: The County Party Committee
            The County Political and Legal Affairs Committee

November 20, 1996
Total number of copies printed: 80

(Note: The original is a handwritten copy. XXX indicates an illegible character.)

ENFORCEMENT PLAN FOR CURBING THE ILLEGAL ACTIVITIES OF THE UNDERGROUND CATHOLIC CHURCH ACCORDING TO LAW

In order conscientiously to implement the Party's policy towards
religion, strengthen the administration of religious affairs in our township,
standardize the conduct of religious activities, and in the light of the actual
conditions in our township, we have decided to take unified action to destroy the
organizational system of the underground Catholic Church, especially in
Shanbei, Leifang and Donglai, and curb the illegal assembly activities. The
specific enforcement plan follows.

I. Guidelines

By publicizing and putting into effect the spirit of the Sixth Plenary
Session of the Party's Fourteenth Congress and "The Decision of the Central
Committee of the Communist Party on Certain Important Questions Concerning
the Strengthening of the Building of Socialist Spiritual Civilization," mobilize
and organize the broad masses, including the religious believers, raise high the
banner of upholding the dignity of law and "running the church independently
by the believers themselves" and the policy of "protecting the legal, curbing the
illegal, and resisting infiltration," as well as the principle of "transformation
through education, divide and disintegrate, unite with the majority and attack the
few," plan carefully, organize well, be resolute, energetic but prudent, so as to
ensure that no blunders are committed. This will ensure that our work to curb
the illegal religious activities according to law proceeds soundly and
successfully, and social stability is promoted.

II. Objectives and Tasks

Destroy the organizational system of the underground Catholic forces in our township. Cut the contacts between those forces and hostile foreign forces and domestic lawless elements. Destroy the illegal places of activity of the church and thoroughly eradicate those religious posters that are openly put up. Strengthen the building of spiritual civilization and grassroots organizations. Popularize laws and statutes, and promote the all-round implementation of the multi-faceted measures to improve public security. Specifically, there are three stages:

(1) The preparatory stage (from November 20 to 25)

A. Establish strong organizations at every level. All personnel should report to duty and start working.

B. Carefully think through and draw up a highly secured enforcement plan, a specific enforcement plan for the township under the unified direction of the county.

C. Working together with the county's work team, organize six work teams to promote spiritual civilization and send them to work in those villages where the underground Catholic forces live in compact communities.

D. Do preparatory work well, draw up a plan for propaganda, tailor the propaganda materials and methods to target different groups: the underground clergy, the backbone elements, the mass of believers. Print announcements of prohibition in the name of the government. Prepare propaganda materials, and unify statements for foreign consumption.

E. Be mentally and spiritually prepared to handle any unexpected incidents. Promptly report any such incident to the superior organs.

(2) The implementation stage (from November 25, 1996 to March 31, 1997)

A. Before November 25, 1996, all spiritual civilization promotion teams must be stationed in villages where the underground Catholic forces and believers live in compact communities. The primary tasks of the teams are XX to launch a large-scale propaganda and educational offensive, making full use of broadcasting and XXX documentary materials, energetically publicize "The Decision of the Central Committee of the Chinese Communist Party on Certain Questions Concerning the Strengthening of the Building of Socialist Spiritual Civilization,, the party's policy towards religion, laws and statutes, and patriotism.

The first thing to do is to secure a firm footing and successfully carry out the work of education and transformation. Members of the work teams must eat, live and work together with the masses and perform good public relations work by visiting every family, engage in heart to heart talks with them and make friends. Sincerely offer them solutions to their practical production problems. And on that basis, try to change their way of thinking and make them work for us. Secondly, make further investigations to achieve an all-round understanding of the basic characteristics of the broad masses of religious believers. Together with the local police stations, develop a complete headcount of the transients and floating population, register and set up a file for each one of them. It is particularly important to investigate and check on those out-of-town believers and gain a clear idea of each and every one of them. In our work, we must fully abide by the law and bring the central role of the grassroots Party organizations into full play. Strengthen the building of the leadership in the villages where religious believers live in compact communities. Evaluate the village Party branches and make necessary adjustments or reinforcements so as to ensure that these Party branches can serve as a fortress in the campaign to curb illegal religious activities.

B. Before November 30, 1996, make a thorough investigation to gain a clear understanding of the underground Catholic clergy, the core members of the religious underground, the number of believers and their illegal activities. Investigate every one of the underground clergy, the XXX believers, especially Party and youth league members, cadres, militiamen, employees and their families, and those who call the believers to the illegal assembly points, find out about their activity schedules, overseas connections, the degrees of stubbornness, the traits that could be taken advantage of, and their psychological characteristics.

C. Develop multi-level education and run the various types of study classes well. The work teams must tailor their education to target different groups. First, for Party members, the study class should be on education in the purpose of the Party. Use the Party constitution to unify the thoughts of Party members, so that they could play the role of the vanguard and serve as a model in the campaign to curb the illegal activities of the underground Catholic forces. Second, the study class for young activists is designed to help them acquire the proletarian life and world outlook, enhance their ability to consciously resist the erosion by all kinds of non-proletarian ideologies, and become a reserve force for the Party's cause. Third, the study class for the clergy and the underground core. Publicize for them the Party's principles and policies, the laws of the land, so that they will know what is consistent with their religious canon and what is unreasonable and unlawful, thereby guiding more and more of them to engage in normal and lawful religious activities.

D. Make a big effort to divide and disintegrate the underground religious forces, educate and unite with the great majority, isolate and crack down on the very few. Conduct positive education and organize a special task force that uses different methods and does everything possible to win over the believers. Justice is on our side, so we must not mince words in explaining the illegality, harmfulness and danger of underground religious activities, as well as the Party and government policy of supporting and protecting the "autonomous church," so that people will understand that the only way out is to run the church autonomously and by themselves. With the exception of a few stubborn core elements who must be placed under strict control, we will deal with the ordinary church members who have violated the law by providing them with education and guidance, and do our best to get them to obey government administration and refrain from illegal religious activities. Those who engage in lawful religious activities, should be provided outlets — appropriate places of worship. In accordance with the principle of uniting with and educating the great majority and isolating the very few, grassroots level cadres and work team members should be assigned tasks to work with specific individuals, persuade them to write statements of repentance, recognize the policy of running the church autonomously and by themselves, and engage in religious activities according to law.

E. Thoroughly eliminate the illegal assembly places according to law. This is to be achieved by conducting mass work in a big way, by relying on the grassroots organizations, and by the power of the masses in settling the religious question as a nonreligious one. Seal those places used for comparatively less serious illegal activities. Have team workers persuade them to register so they could engage in lawful religious activities, and be brought under normal administration. At the same time, underground monasteries and convents, once discovered, must be firmly suppressed.

F. Firmly ban large-scale illegal assembly activities as on "*December 25.*" First, place the underground clergy and core elements in our township under control and prevent them from participating in illegal activities. Second, in every village where believers live in compact communities, exits must be effectively blocked. Believers must be firmly persuaded not to leave their township or village. Third, preparations and publicity work must be done early. Licenses and permits for vehicles and equipment used for religious activities are to be revoked and their users fined. At the same time, preparations must be made to handle emergencies.

G. Control the schools, adjust and strengthen the teaching staff in villages where believers live in compact communities. Teachers who engage in illegal religious activities must be reassigned or even dismissed. Strict rules must he instituted banning any missionary activities in schools. Ban all organized study, observation and visitation of any form of religious activity. Students are not allowed to carry any religious symbols or propaganda materials. All violators must be dealt with severely. Other activities that interfere with the administration and family planning in the name of religion must be firmly curbed. Cases arc to be dealt with according to their seriousness.

By carrying out the above described measures, we should be able basically to destroy the organizational system of the underground Catholic forces in our township, their assembly places, and divide and disintegrate the underground Catholic forces, prevent the underground religious forces and believers from participating in the large-scale illegal assembly activities at Shitangshan, cut their contact with domestic lawless elements and hostile foreign forces, so that our township's work on religion is becoming gradually standardized and religious affairs are administered according to law.

Ill. The Stage of Consolidation (from April 1, 1997 to June 30, 1997)
To consolidate our achievements in the special struggle and prevent relapses, we must regard the special struggle to curb illegal Catholic activities according to law as a political task and persist in it on a long-term basis. This concentrated and unified action requires three months for consolidation. We need to work hard on comprehensive control and pick the right time to launch a second wave of offensive, firmly ban the illegal assembly of the underground Catholic forces in our township. The villages must also strengthen institution building, draw up village rules and popular compacts.

IV. Organization and Leadership
Establish the "Donglai Township Leadership Team for Curbing the illegal Activities of Underground Catholic Forces."

Team leader: Yang Shusen; Deputy team leader: Chen Zemin, Members: Li Xianchang, Xiong Xiaoqiu, Huang Lusun, Xiao Jingxing, Chen Guimin, Lu Yaomin, Huang Rongshun, Sun Guangrong, XXX Kaiwu, Huang Xinmin;. Office manager Huang Xinmin.

V. Matters Demanding Attention
(1) Having a good grasp of policies, being particular about tactics, and strict adherence to the law. Leaders at various levels must regard the work of

curbing illegal activities as an important "engineering" project for strengthening spiritual construction and managing society. Strategically, we must be resolute and seize the initiative; tactically, we must be energetic and prudent. Handle political issues as non-political issues, and religious issues as non-religious issues. Avoid sharpening the contradictions by inappropriate methods and avoid the introduction of destabilizing factors, popular disturbances and other serious incidents.

(2) Discipline must be strictly observed; commands must be obeyed. All decisions made by the county and township leadership must be resolutely carried out. Dereliction of duty caused by negligence must be investigated and dealt with gravely. The system of reporting for instructions and feedback must be strictly enforced. The work teams must report to the township leadership on the progress in their work every week. At the same time, secrets must be kept. Do not disclose anything that should not be disclosed. [For] disclosure of secrets that unfavorably affect the campaign, the culprit must be punished by dismissal. If the offense is serious, the offender will be criminally prosecuted according to law.

(3) A strict responsibility system must be enforced. The village committees and units must, in the light of local conditions, assign specific tasks and responsibilities to individuals. Disobedience of orders and taboos, irresponsibility or shifting responsibility onto others resulting in missed strategic opportunity with serious consequences must be conclusively investigated. Village committees and units directly under the township must take the initiative to coordinate their efforts, and successfully carry out the difficult and glorious tasks assigned them by the Party's county committee and the county government.

Donglal Township Leadership Group for Curbing the Illegal Activities of the Catholic Church According to Law

November 20, 1996

Slogans of the Special Struggle to Curb Illegal Activities Donglai Township

1. All religious activities must be conducted within the constitution, laws and regulations and with the permission of policy!
2. Energetically carry out the special struggle to curb the illegal religious activities according to law!
3. Firmly curb and crack down on unlawful and criminal activities conducted in the name of religion!

4. Firmly curb and crack down on illegal missionary activities and unlawful assemblies!

5. It is forbidden to provide sites and supplies for illegal religious activities. Violators will be severely punished!

6. It is forbidden to host out-of-town believers. Violators will be punished severely!

7. Protect the lawful, curb the unlawful, and crack down on the violators!

8. It is forbidden to go to Yujiashan, Shitanshan and Zengjia to attend meetings. Violators will be severely punished!

9. It is forbidden to engage in activities at sites of illegal religious activities not approved by the government!

10. Firmly ban all sites of illegal religious activities!

Donglai Township Spiritual Enrichment Propaganda Team (Membership List)

Shanbei Village Committee
        Group leader: Li Xianchang
        Deputy group leader: Xiao Jingxing
        Members: Chen Zhengsun, Zhou Xiaoqiu, Li Yonggen

Leifang Village Committee
        Group leader: Xiong Xiaoqiu
        Deputy group leader: Chen Guimin
        Members: Le Guixiu, Zheng Xiaoping, Sun Guangrong

Donglai Village Committee
        Group leader: Huang Lusun
        Deputy group leader: Chen Zeming
        Members: Luo Chunfa, Deng Dongyu, Zeng Yonggao

Tangren Village Committee
        Group leader: Huang Rongshun
        Member: X Shuiming

Chenjia Village Committee
        Group leader: Lu Aiming
        Member: Yuan Axing

Caching Village Committee
        Group leader: Zhou Kaiwu
        Member: Dai Xinsheng

Donglai Township's Work Plan for "Curbing Illegal Activities"

Propaganda and Mobilization Stage (November 20-25, 1996)
1. Township Party committee and government convene a meeting to discuss and plan the work for "curbing illegal activities"; draw up an enforcement plan;
2. Township government calls a meeting of all party cadres in the township;
3. Township committee convenes meetings of Party branch committees, and of Party members, and holds a mass rally;
4. Village committee sets up subgroups;
5. All village committees and units put up permanent slogans (two or three slogans per village group.

Investigation Stage (November 26-30)
1. Investigate and ascertain the population of religious believers;
2. Locate and ascertain the number of key village committees (thirty or more Catholic families) and key households (two or more believers);
3. Find out all about the sites of activities (meaning assembly sites);
4. Prepare a list of the underground Catholic clergy and core members; investigate and find out all about their routine activities and criminal deeds.

Education and Transformation Stage (December 1-15)
I. Prepare propaganda materials; ready the "three courses" on the policy towards religion; laws and regulations; and the building of spiritual civilization;
2. Start study classes for the believers;
3. Hold mass rallies and educate the believers according to their different levels;
4. Draw up village rules and popular compacts;
5. Village committees and village groups sign papers of responsibility;
6. Clearly define the system of helping and educating the believers, and sign papers of guarantee;
7. Strengthen the building of grassroots Party branches and grassroots governments.

Legal Control Stage (December 16-31)
1. Block the exits and ensure that no one leaves the village or the township on December 25;

2. Prevent out-of-towners from entering the township;
3. Strengthen monitoring and control;
4. Ban and seal all illegal religious assembly sites;
5. Strictly outlaw illegal assembly activities in the various types of schools.

Consolidation and Summing Up Stage (January-June 30, 1997)
1. Consolidate the achievements of the work to "curb illegal activities"; carry on the special struggle to curb illegal religious activities according to law on a long-term basis and as a political task;
2. Strengthen the building of institutions; form a permanent religious surveillance group;
3. Successfully sum up and evaluate our work.

APPENDIX IV: REGULATIONS FROM THE SHANGHAI RELIGIOUS AFFAIRS BUREAU

(Approved on Nov. 30, 1995 by the Standing Committee of the Shanghai 10th People's Congress at its 23rd Meeting)

Announcements from the Standing Committee of the Shanghai People's Congress

Number 35

Herein are issued "Regulations from the Shanghai Religious Affairs Bureau," approved by the Standing Committee of the 10th People's Congress of Shanghai. These regulations will take effect on March 1, 1996.

Shanghai People's Congress Standing Committee December 1995

Chapter 1:   **General Principles**

Article 1:   These regulations are formulated to safeguard the freedom of religious belief of our citizens, to maintain lawful supervision over religious affairs, to preserve the country's unity and union among her citizens, to defend social stability, and to promote the building of a modern socialist society. They are based on the Constitution of the People's Republic of China, and other relevant laws and regulations applying them to specific conditions in Shanghai.

Article 2:   All citizens have freedom of religious belief. No organization or individual should discriminate against citizens who believe in religion or those who do not believe. All citizens should respect each other, regardless of religious faith or lack of it, and regardless of differing religious beliefs.

Article 3:   The term *religion* in these regulations refers to: Buddhism, Daoism, Islamism, Catholicism and Protestantism.

Article 4:   The term *religious affairs* in these regulations refers to all common social activities that take place between religion and the state, society or the masses.

Article 5:   The lawful rights of religious communities, their normal religious activities and places for these activities are protected by law. These rights are exercised within the limits permitted by the Constitution, and other laws and regulations. No organization or individual should use religion to carry out illegal activities.

Article 6:   The principle that religion should not interfere in government administration, judicial procedures, school and public education must be firmly maintained. In order to safeguard the nation's sovereignty, and the principle of independent, autonomous administration, no foreign power is to control religious organization and their affairs.

Article 7:   The Religious Affairs Bureau of the Shanghai Municipal People's Government is the principal administrative bureau for religious affairs in Shanghai.

The Religious Affairs Bureaus of the District and County levels of the People's Government are the principal administrative bureaus for religious affairs for districts and counties, and implement directions from the Religious Affairs Bureau of the Shanghai People's Government.

The Municipal, District and County Religious Affairs Bureaus have the duty to inspect, direct, assist and supervise the full implementation of these regulations in Shanghai and those areas under its jurisdiction.

All other pertinent departments in the municipal government should implement these regulations according to their own respective responsibilities.

Article 8:   National government agencies, enterprises, businesses, social organizations and individuals in Shanghai should also implement and follow these regulations.

Chapter 2:   Religious Organizations
Article 9:   The religious organization that these regulations refer to are those lawfully established; namely, The Shanghai Buddhist Association, The Shanghai Catholic Patriotic Association, The Shanghai Catholic Diocese, The Shanghai Catholic Administrative Committee, The Shanghai Protestant 3-Self Patriotic Movement, The Shanghai Protestant Christian Council and other religious organizations lawfully constituted in Shanghai and those districts and counties under its jurisdiction.

Article 10:   Religious organizations must register according to the State Council's *Administrative Regulations Governing the Registration of Social Organizations*. Religious activities are permitted only after approval is obtained from the registration bureau. Persons meeting the law's qualifications for juridical persons are then recognized as such.

Article 11:   Religious organizations must obey the Constitution, laws, and regulations, and accept government supervision.

Religious organizations, while maintaining their aims and developing activities which accord with their own respective constitutions, must assist the government to fully implement its pertinent laws and regulations on religion, promote patriotism, socialism and education in government legal systems among its own clergy and believers; safeguard their legal rights; organize or help in organizing normal religious activities.

Article 12:   Religious organizations can promote religious cultural studies and exchanges. Publishing, printing and distribution of religious books, articles and videos must be carried out in accord with pertinent regulations.

Article 13:   Friendly contacts between Shanghai religious organizations with those of Taiwan, Hong Kong and Macau should follow the principles of non-subordination, non-interference and mutual respect.

Article 14:   Religious organizations, (including places for religious activities) may apply to operate business enterprises according to pertinent government regulations for the purpose of self-support. They may also operate enterprises that benefit public welfare.

Chapter 3:   Religious Personnel
Article 15:   Persons whom these regulations term religious personnel include the following: Buddhist monks and nuns, Daoist priests and nuns, Islamic imams, Catholic bishops, priests, seminarians (religious) and sisters, Protestant bishops, ministers, presbyters and catechists.

Article 16:   The identity of religious personnel is established by the Shanghai religious organizations according to their own regulations. These names of these persons are in turn entered into the files of the municipal Religious Affairs Bureau.

Article 17:   Religious personnel registered and acknowledged as such can perform religious activities in lawfully registered places for religious worship. The legitimate rights of these personnel are protected by law.

Article 18:   Shanghai religious personnel who are invited to other parts of the country or religious personnel from other areas in China who come to Shanghai to perform or take charge of religious activities, must first seek approval from the local religious organizations and register at the municipal Religious Affairs Bureau.

Chapter 4:   **Places for Religious Activities**

Article 19:   The places where local citizens carry out their religious activities and to which these regulations refer are as follows: Buddhist and Daoist temples, Islamic mosques, Catholic and Protestant churches and other places that have been established for religious activities.

Article 20:   Establishment of places for religious activities must be in accord with the State Council's Regulations for the Management of Places for Religious Activity. Application should be made to the Religious Affairs Bureau above the District and County levels. After obtaining approval according to the Procedure for the Registration of Places for Religious Activity, registration should be carried out under the name of a qualified juridical person, after which a certificate of registration will be issued to said juridical person.

Article 21:   Places for religious activity must have a management committee, carry out a democratic management program, set up a sound management system and accept administrative supervision from the pertinent government departments.

Article 22:   Places for religious activities that close down, join others, move or change their registration, must go through formalities at the original place of registration. For those places that close down, their properties must be handled according to the pertinent government regulations.

Article 23:   Places for religious activities may accept voluntary donations in the form of alms, offerings, subsidies and other gifts (including legacies) from individuals or organizations.

For gifts from foreign individuals or organizations the pertinent regulations must be observed.

Article 24:   The managing committee of places for religious activities may sell religious articles, religious works of art and legally published religious books and periodicals as well as religious videos.

Article 25:   Without authorization of the management committee and the Religious Affairs Bureau no unit or individual may set up a business or service center in a place for religious activities, carry on business or set up exhibition or displays.

Article 26:   Filming movies or TV programs in places for religious activities must have the approval of the management committee and the authorization of the Religious Affairs Bureau.

Article 27:   Non-religious units are not permitted to build temples, churches, or other religious facilities or to organize any religious activities.
Places not set aside for religious activities and non religious organizations may not accept alms, donations or offerings, and gifts of a religious nature either openly or in secret.

Article 28:   Such activities as divination, fortune telling, palm reading, casting of lots, exorcisms and healings are not permitted in places for religious activities.

Chapter 5:   **Religious Activities**
Article 29:   Religious activities can be carried out only in places registered for religious activities and authorized by the Religious Affairs Bureau.

Article 30:   Religious believers may perform religious activities according to their respective rites, rules and customs in places for religious worship. These include: worshiping Buddha, recitation of prayers, reconciliation services, following a vegetarian diet, fasting, prayer, Sunday services, Bible sharing, preaching, Baptism, celebrating Mass, anointing the sick, requiem services, observing feast days, etc. One can also practice religion at home.

Article 31:   The public celebration of religious activities must be performed by religious personnel or those who meet the required criteria.

Article 32:   No organization or individual may propagate in places for religious worship a faith or religion different from that being practiced there, nor may they engage in religious debates. No one may preach religion outside of places set aside for religious activities.

Article 33:   Religious activities should not disturb the social order, the forces of production nor should it harm people's health.

Article 34:   Marriage services can be performed in places for religious activity after the parties have registered at the Marriage Registration Office.

Chapter 6:   Religious Institutes
Article 35:   Religious institutes should be operated by municipal religious organizations and application for registration should be made, according to regulations, to the concerned department.

Article 36:   Enrollment in religious institutes must be strictly carried out according to enrollment conditions; namely, that candidates apply of their own free will, are recommended by the local religious communities and are selected through an examination process.

Article 37:   Religious institutes must maintain tight control over their internal management and be ready to accept the supervision and directions of the concerned government departments.

Article 38:   Local students as well as those from other areas outside Shanghai who enroll in local religious institutes can take the local religious institute as their place of residence.
      Students coming from other areas outside Shanghai who with reason quit the course half way through or after graduation do not carry out their ministry in Shanghai must have their place of residence transferred from the city.

Article 39:   The main source of funds for the expenses of religious institutes will come from their own religious communities.

Chapter 7:   Religious Property
Article 40:   By religious properties are meant real estate, buildings, various kinds of equipment and tools, art work, cultural artifacts belonging to religious communities, income from religious sources, all donations and enterprises as well as all other lawful possession of goods and income that belong to a religious community or to places of religious activity or are under its control and use.

Article 41:   The property that religious organizations or places for religious activity possess, control or use are protected by law and should not be expropriated by other organizations or individuals.

Article 42:   Religious real estate must be registered by the religious organizations or places of religious worship in Shanghai according to the concerned regulations at the department for house registrations at the city, district or county levels. A certificate of registration will be given attesting to the right of ownership. Should any changes occur, registration of such changes should be made as soon as possible and recorded at the Shanghai Religious Affairs Bureau.

Article 43: If places for religious activities or religious structures are designated as cultural relics or examples of excellent modern architecture, or important and prominent religious locations that should be preserved, then the boundaries of these protected areas, where construction will be controlled, must be clearly designated in all city planning. Any construction in these areas must conform to concerned regulations.

Without the approval of the Municipal Planning Department and the Religious Affairs Bureau of Shanghai, these above mentioned places cannot be changed into other uses.

Article 44: When a place for religious activities must be demolished owing to definite needs of urban development, approval must first be obtained from the religious organizations in question and the Religious Affairs Bureau. Another piece of property of the same dimensions as well as suitable compensations must be provided for reconstruction.

Article 45: When any real estate of a religious organization must be demolished or put to other use owing to needs of urban development, approval must first be obtained from the pertinent religious communities or management committees of places for religious activity and the Religious Affairs Bureau, and a written agreement must be given to said organizations along with reasonable compensation and an appropriate settlement.

Article 46: Houses belonging to religious organizations or places for religious activity can rent their property according to pertinent regulations. Both landlord and tenant must draw up a contract binding in law. If the tenant violates the contract, the landlord has the right to terminate the contract and withdraw the tenant's right of use.

Chapter 8: Foreign Contacts
Article 47: Religious organizations or individuals in Shanghai who have contact with foreign religious persons to engage in friendly exchanges and share cultural activities must insist on the principles of independence, autonomy, mutual respect, non-interference, equality and friendship.

Article 48:   Religious communities or individuals in Shanghai invited to go abroad for religious purposes or who invite foreign organizations or individuals to visit China must go through the formalities according to concerned regulations.

Article 49:   Places for religious activities in Shanghai or places recognized as such by the Religious Affairs Bureau may receive foreigners to take part in religious activities and may permit them upon request to celebrate Daoist or Buddhist rites, baptisms, marriages, funerals and other religious rites.
          Foreigners may also, upon invitation from religious organizations, preach and lead prayers in places for religious activity in Shanghai.

Article 50:   Foreigners who wish to film movies or TV videos in places for religious activity in Shanghai must first obtain approval from the management committee of the said places, as well as from the Shanghai Film and TV Administration Department and the Shanghai Religious Affairs Bureau.

Article 51:   Foreigners entering China may, according to Chinese immigration regulations, bring in for their own personal use small quantities of printed religious materials, audio and video tapes and other religious articles.

Article 52:   Foreigners who perform religious activities in Shanghai must obey Chinese laws and regulations. They are not allowed to establish religious organizations or religious office, set up places for religious activity or religious institutes. They should not seek to increase the number of believers among Chinese citizens, appoint any religious personnel, distribute religious propaganda, audio or video tapes or do any other evangelizing activities.

Article 53:   Concerned government departments in Shanghai that deal with foreigners in the fields of economy, culture, education, health, sports and in other exchange programs, must not accept any attached religious conditions.

Chapter 9:   Legal Responsibilities
Article 54:   Should infringements of these regulations constitute a violation of the PRC Public Security Administration Penal Code, punishment will be meted out by the Public Security organs according to established penalties. If they violate National Safety Laws of the People's Republic of China or other laws and regulations, they must be dealt with by the pertinent agencies according to the established penalties. Should the violation constitute a crime, the judicial agencies should investigate and affix criminal responsibility.

Article 55:   For infringements of these regulations the Religious Affairs Bureau or concerned agencies, should mete out penalties according to the gravity of the matter at hand. They may dissuade or prevent the parties concerned from carrying out illegal activities, give warnings, issue commands to cease and desist, temporally disband the organization, revoke the registration, or suppress it altogether, order a restoration of the former situation or impose a fine, or confiscate illegal structures, facilities, religious propaganda or income. They can also impose on religious organizations a fine above 1000 RMB and below 50,000 RMB and for individuals directly responsible they can impose a fine above 50 RMB and below 500 RMB.

Article 56:   When the Administrative Department decides the punishment to be meted out, a written document is to be issued on the matter. When a fine is received, an official receipt issued by the Municipal Finance Department for said purpose should be issued. The fine must be paid to the Finance Department according to regulations.

Article 57:   Should the concerned person not agree to the said administrative decision, he may according to the Regulations for Reviewing Administrative Decisions or the Criminal Procedure Law request a review of the decision or initiate legal proceedings.

Article 58:   Should violators of the present regulations be Chinese citizens they are to be punished according to the concerned regulations or by the unit where they are working.

Article 59:   Should violators of the present regulations be foreigners, the Religious Affairs Bureau or other concerned agencies must dissuade and prevent the party's actions. Should their actions constitute a violation of immigration policy concerning foreigners entering and leaving the country, or a violation of security measures, the Public Security Bureau should deal with the matter according to the regulations. Should they constitute a crime, the judicial agencies should investigate and affix criminal responsibility.

Chapter 10: Supplementary Articles
Article 60:   Overseas Chinese or residents of Taiwan, Hong Kong and Macau carrying out religious activities in Shanghai must abide by these regulations.

Article 61: The Government Municipal Religious Affairs Bureau can implement detailed rules based on these regulations with the approval of the city government.

Article 62: The Shanghai Religious Affairs Bureau is responsible for explanations on how these regulations are to be implemented.

Article 63: These regulations are effective from March 1, 1996.

(Translation from *Tripod*, Volume XVI, No. 92.)

APPENDIX V: *EXCERPTS FROM* QUESTIONS AND ANSWERS ON THE PATRIOTIC EDUCATION PROGRAM IN MONASTERIES

Question 1

What is the reason for establishing normal order in the monasteries through patriotic education, weeding out, and reforms?

Answer

It is to continue the policy concerning the unification of the motherland, the promotion of political stability, the strengthening of the solidarity of the nationalities, and the struggles to oppose separatists activities, in order to establish a socialist system with Chinese characteristics. There is no question of choice or scope for falling out of step but to join and follow the forward march of the nationalities of the great family of the motherland.

Question 2

What are the contents of the "Four Points" as defined by Comrade Li Ruihuan concerning the Dalai?

Answer

The Dalai is:

a. the head of the serpent and the chieftain of the group [seeking] splittism and Tibetan independence.

b. a loyal tool of the international anti-China forces.

c. the root cause of stirring up social turmoil in Tibet.

d. the biggest obstacle standing in the way of establishing normal order in Tibetan Buddhism

Question 4

What are the four cardinal devotions to be assimilated by the monk and nun population?

Answer

a. devotion to the motherland

b. devotion to the government

c. devotion to the law

d. devotion to citizenship

Question 6

What are normal religious practices and what are irreligious practices ?

Answer

a. Saying prayers, doing prostrations and reciting scriptural texts, burning incense, attending religious teachings and celebrating religious festivals are all normal religious practices.

b. Any action that is prompted by ignorance and superstition, that undermines the interest of the State and peoples' lives and property are examples of irreligious practice.

100

Question 7   What are the aims of the Party's implementation of the policy of freedom of religious belief and the strengthening of supervision of religious activities in accordance with the law ?

Answer   To give guidance and leadership to the adaptation of religion to the socialist system.

Question 13   What separatist activities have the Dalai clique instigated ?

Answer   The main separatist activities are:

a. instigating the violent rebellion of 1959.

b. the establishment of a government in exile and the establishment of a force to instigate rebellion and disturbances.

c. resorting to western hostile powers to clandestinely promote the idea of Tibetan independence in the international fora through deceitful propaganda, thereby damaging the international reputation and image of our country.

d. intensifying the effort to infiltrate areas within the Tibet Autonomous Region to plan and instigate disturbances; and sabotaging the search and recognition of the reincarnation of the Tenth Panchen Lama, and engaging in intimidation.

Question 14   Who is the chief backer of the Dalai clique? Without the backing, could the Dalai clique survive?

Answer   The Dalai clique assiduously seeks the support and backing of the Western capitalists. Without Western support, there is no way the Dalai clique could survive.

Question 17   What is the position of Tibet vis a vis the fundamental interests of the nationalities of the People's Republic of China ?

Answer   There are two points:

a. From the overall strategic viewpoint the peace and security of Tibet is linked to the sovereignty as well as the peace and security of the entire State.

b. The issue of stability, peace and security, and development of Tibet are matters that can only be addressed from within the great family of the motherland.

Question 19   What kind of person should be entrusted with the leadership responsibility and authority of the monasteries ?

Answer   The leadership responsibility and authority of the monasteries
                  should definitely be entrusted in the hands of monks and nuns
                  who are genuine law-abiding patriots

Question 23.   What fundamental rights and duties are enshrined in the
                  Constitution for the citizens of our country?

Answer   All citizens have rights and freedoms that are enshrined in the
                  constitution. The fundamental rights are:
                  a. right to equality;
                  b. right to political freedom;
                  c. right to religious freedom;
                  d. right to life;
                  e. right to make criticisms, put forward proposals for discussion,
                  make representations concerning one's case, make appeals to
                  courts or to expose others' wrongdoing, and to obtain
                  compensation for losses;
                  f. right to a share in the social economy;
                  g. right to education;
                  h. protection of the rights and interests of women of the country;
                  i. right to protection by the state for married families, the
                  elderly, and the pregnant.

                  The duties of the citizens are:
                   a. to defend and protect the unity of the country and the
                  solidarity of the nationalities;
                   b. to respect and defend the constitution and the basic laws,
                  safeguard thoroughly state secrets, protect public property,
                  observe labour discipline and public order, and preserve the
                  general moral behaviour of society;
                  c. to defend and protect the security and honour and interests of
                  the country;
                  d. to defend and protect the motherland, and in accordance with
                  the law, voluntarily enlist in the People's Militia;
                  e. to labour which is the glorious duty and responsibility of all
                  workers endowed with the strength to work;
                  f. to pay taxes as provided for in the constitution; and
                  g. to implement the family planning programme.

Question 24.   What constitutes a "crime" ?

Answer   Committing a 'crime' means :

a. any action and behaviour that is offensive and harmful to society;

b. any action and behavior that violates the criminal law; and

c. any action and behavior that deserves to be punished.

by the Work Team of the Patriotic Education Program in Yartoe township, Nedong county, May 25,1997

(Document and translation from Tibet Information Network, London.)

APPENDIX VI: REGULATIONS ON THE SUPERVISION OF THE RELIGIOUS ACTIVITIES OF FOREIGNERS IN CHINA

Order of the State Council of the People's Republic of China

No. 144

The "Regulations on the Supervision of the Religious Activities of Foreigners in China," is now issued and comes into force on the day of issue.
(signed by) Premier Li Peng, January 31, 1994.

Article 1:   To safeguard foreigners' freedom of religious belief within the borders of the People's Republic of China, and to maintain and protect society's public interests, these regulations have been formulated in accordance with the constitution.

Article 2:   The People's Republic of China respects the freedom of religious belief of foreigners who stay within China's borders, and protects foreigners who have friendly contacts, as well as cultural and academic exchanges with their religious counterparts in China as regards religion.

Article 3:   Foreigners may attend religious activities within China's borders at places for religious activities, such as monasteries, temples, mosques and churches. When invited by religious bodies at or above provincial, autonomous regional, or municipal level, foreigners may lecture on scripture and give sermons at religious places in China.

Article 4:   Foreigners may carry out religious activities to be attended by foreigners at places sanctioned by religious affairs bodies of the People's Government at or above county level.

Article 5:   Foreigners who stay within China's borders may invite religious personnel in China to conduct religious ceremonies for them, such as baptisms, marriages, funerals, and Daoist and Buddhist rites.

Article 6:   Foreigners who enter China may carry religious publications, religious audiovisual material and other religious articles for their own use; when the amount of religious publications, religious audio-visual material and other religious articles brought across the border is greater than for personal use, this matter must be dealt with according to the relevant customs regulations of China.

Religious publications and religious audio-visual products whose contents endanger Chinese society's public interests are banned from entering China.

Article 7: Foreigners within China's borders who recruit candidates to go abroad to be trained as religious personnel, or who study or teach at religious institutes in China, must be dealt with according to the relevant regulations of China.

Article 8: Foreigners within China's borders who conduct religious activities must observe Chinese laws and regulations; they are not allowed to establish religious organizations, set up religious offices, open places for religious activities or run religious institutes, nor may they develop followers, appoint religious personnel or conduct missionary activities among Chinese citizens.

Article 9: If foreigners engage in religious activities that violate these regulations, religious affairs bodies and other relevant departments of the People's Government at or above county level should dissuade or stop them. For foreigners whose behavior violates immigration rules or the administration of public security, punishment will be meted out by public security bodies according to the law. If a crime is committed, responsibility for the crime will be investigated and judged by judiciary bodies according to the law.

Article 10: These regulations apply to foreign organizations whose religious activities take place within the borders of the People's Republic of China.

Article 11: Reference should be made to these regulations regarding religious activities conducted within China's borders by Chinese citizens who reside outside China, as well as by Taiwan, Hong Kong and Macau residents.

Article 12: These regulations are subject to the interpretation of the Bureau of Religious Affairs under the State Council.

Article 13: These regulations should be implemented from the day they are issued.

(Translation from *China News and Church Report*.)

APPENDIX VII: REGULATIONS REGARDING THE MANAGEMENT OF PLACES OF RELIGIOUS ACTIVITIES

Order of the State Council of the People's Republic of China

No. 145

The *Regulations Regarding the Management of Places of Religious Activity* is now issued and comes into force on the day of issue.

(signed by) Premier Li Peng, January 31, 1994.

Article 1: To protect normal religious activities, maintain and safeguard the legal rights of places for religious activities, and facilitate the administration of places for religious activities, these regulations have been formulated in accordance with the constitution.

Article 2: Places for religious activities referred to in these regulations are places where religious activities are held—monasteries, temples, mosques, churches and other fixed locations.

To establish a place for religious activities, it is necessary to go through a registration process. The method of registration is determined by the Bureau of Religious Affairs under the State Council.

Article 3: Each place for religious activities is run independently by its own management body. Its legal rights and normal religious activities are protected by law. No organizations or individuals are allowed to violate and interfere with them.

Article 4: Places for religious activities must establish their own administrative system. Laws and regulations must be observed when religious activities are conducted at such places. No one may use these places to engage in activities that harm national unity, the solidarity of ethnic groups, social stability or the physical health of citizens, or obstruct the state educational system.

Places for religious activities are not subject to control by organizations and individuals outside the borders of China.

Article 5: Anyone who often stays at places for religious activities as well as people who do not belong to such places but temporarily stay in them must observe state regulations regarding household registration.

106

Article 6:   Places for religious activities may accept alms, offerings and *niyah* (donation from Muslims) voluntarily contributed by their faithful.

         In accepting donations from organizations and individuals outside China's borders, places for religious activities must act in accordance with relevant state regulations.

Article 7:   Management bodies of places for religious activities may, in accordance with relevant state regulations, sell religious articles, religious artwork, and religious books and periodicals at their respective places.

Article 8:   The property and income of a place for religious activities are to be administered and used by its own management body. No other units and individuals are allowed to seize or transfer them gratuitously.

Article 9:   If a place for religious activities closes down or is integrated with others, this fact should be reported to the original registry. The property is to by dealt with according to state regulations.

Article 10:   In order for a place for religious activities to manage and use lands, hills and forests, houses, etc., a certificate must be obtained by its own management body or an affiliated religious group in accordance with relevant state regulations.

         If the state requisitions lands, hills and forests, houses, etc., that are managed and used by the places for religious activities, this matter should be handled in accordance with the *Law for the Administration of the Land of the People's Republic of China* and other relevant state regulations.

Article 11:   If a unit or individual is to rebuild a house or construct a new building, set up a commercial enterprise or service network, hold activities such as a display or exhibition, or make a movie or television program within the area managed by the places for religious activities, approval first must be obtained from the management body of that place and from religious affairs bodies of the People's Government at or above county level, before going to the appropriate department to fulfill procedural requirements.

Article 12:   Places for religious activities listed as protected cultural relics or located within famous scenic areas should manage and protect the cultural relics and environment, and accept the guidance and supervision of relevant departments, according to relevant laws and regulations.

Article 13:   Implementation of these regulations is subject to the guidance and supervision of the religious affairs bodies of the People's Government at or above the county level.

Article 14:   If places for religious activities violate stipulations of these regulations, the religious affairs bodies of the People's Government at or above the county level may, depending on the seriousness of the case, give a warning, stop the activities, or cancel the registration as punishment; but specially serious situations would be passed on to the People's Government at the same level to issue a ban (to the places) in accordance with the law.

Article 15:   Those who break this ordinance and whose behavior is sufficient to violate the management of public security will be punished by public security bodies in accordance with the *Regulations on Punishment and Administration of Public Security of the People's Republic of China.* If a crime is committed, responsibility for the crime will be investigated and judged by judiciary bodies according to law.

Article 16:   If the people concerned disagree with administrative decisions on handling a case, they can, based on laws and regulation, apply for administrative re-examination or else initiate an administrative appeal.

Article 17:   If there is a violation of the stipulations of these regulations and infringement on the legal rights of the places for religious activities, the religious affairs bodies of the People's Government at or above the county level can seek an order from the People's Government at the same level to stop the infringing activities; economic losses that may be incurred should be compensated according to law.

Article 18:   The People's Government at provincial, autonomous regional and municipal level may, based on these regulations and in connection with the actual local situation, formulate ways to implement these regulations.

Article 19:   These regulations are subject to interpretation by the Bureau of Religious Affairs under the State Council.

Article 20:   These regulations should be implemented from the day they are issued.

(Translation from *China News and Church Report.*)

APPENDIX VIII: REGISTRATION PROCEDURES FOR VENUES FOR RELIGIOUS ACTIVITIES

Article 1:   These Procedures are formulated in accordance with Article 2 of the "Regulations Regarding the Management of Places of Religious Activities" [Document No.145].

Article 2:   The following conditions must be met to establish a venue for religious activity:
1) there must be a fixed place and name.
2) there must be citizens who are religious believers who regularly take part in religious activities.
3) there must be a management organization composed of citizens who are religious believers.
4) there must be professional clergy or persons who meet the requirements of the particular religious group to conduct religious services.
5) there must be a legal source of income.

Article 3:   At the time of application for registration, the venue for religious activity must provide the following documentation:
1) an application form.
2) documentation and credentials related to the venue.
3) the opinion of the village (or township) People's Government or of the city neighborhood committee.

Article 4:   The head of the venue's management organization must submit the application for registration, together with the materials required under Article 3, to the Religious Affairs Department of the People's Government at the county level or above.

Article 5:   Upon receipt of an application for registration and related materials, the Religious Affairs Department of the People's Government at the county level or above must make a decision on whether to consider the application within 15 days, on the basis of whether the materials are complete.

Article 6:   The Religious Affairs Department of the People's Government at the county level or above will, within sixty days of the decision to consider the application, grant registration and issue a registration certificate to those venues which, based upon investigation and the opinions of related parties, comply with the regulations found in Articles 2 and 3 of these Procedures, and with related

109

provisions in the "Regulations Regarding the Management of Places of Religious Activities." Venues which do not fully comply with the regulations will, upon review, be granted temporary registration or deferred registration or be denied registration. They will be notified in writing and given an explanation for the decision.

Article 7:   Religious venues registered before the promulgation of these Procedures must exchange their certificate; those which have not been registered should apply for registration according to these Procedures.

Article 8:   If a religious venue closes, merges, moves or otherwise changes the terms which applied at the time of application, its management organization must apply for modification of the certificate to the original issuing body.

Article 9:   According to the regulations of the "General Civil Law," legally registered venues for religious activities which qualify as juridical persons and which at the same time apply to register as juridical persons, will be issued a certificate of registration as juridical persons. According to the law, a religious venue as a juridical person independently enjoys civil rights and takes on civil responsibilities.

Article 10:   A venue's certificate of registration and certificate of registration as a juridical person cannot be changed, transferred or lent. If the certificate is lost, the venue should report its loss promptly to the original issuing body and apply for a replacement.

Article 11:   Upon being granted registration, a venue for religious activity must submit an annual management report to the Religious Affairs Department of the government during the first quarter of each year.

Article 12:   The certificate of registration for venues of religious activities and related forms will be uniform and will be issued by the Religious Affairs Bureau of the State Council.

Article 13:   Matters not regulated by these Procedures follow the "Regulations Regarding the Management of Places of Religious Activities."

Article 14:   Interpretation of these Procedures is the provenance of the Religious Affairs Bureau of the State Council.

Article 15:   These Procedures take effect from the date of promulgation.

1 May 1994

(Translation from *China News and Church Report*.)

APPENDIX IX: METHOD FOR THE ANNUAL INSPECTION
OF PLACES OF RELIGIOUS ACTIVITY

Article 1: In order to protect the legal rights of places of religious activity, strengthen the management of places of religious activity according to law, and advance the systemization and standardization of the self-management of places of religious activity, this Method is established according to the relevant regulations of the Management of Places of Religious Activity Ordinance and the Method of Registration for Places of Religious Activity.

Article 2: This Method applies to places of religious activity registered according to the law with the religious affairs departments of People's Governments at county level or above.

Article 3: The department responsible for the annual inspection of a place of religious activity is the department which is responsible for the registration of that place of religious activity.

Article 4: The main criteria of the annual inspection of a place of religious activity are:
a. The situation as to obedience to national law, regulations and policies;
b. The situation as to the establishment and implementation of management regulations;
c. The situation regarding the main religious and foreign-related activities;
d. The situation regarding important matters of financial management, income and expenditure;
e. The situation regarding any changes in the conditions of registration;
f. The situation as to the changes and management of any business, enterprises or estates (belonging to the place of religious activity);
g. The situation as to any other relevant matters.

Article 5: The departments responsible for the annual inspection shall carry out the annual inspection of the management situation of the places of religious activity according to law in the first quarter of the year. The departments responsible for the annual inspection shall inform the management organizations of the places of religious activity in writing and in advance of the content, time and concrete requirements.

Article 6: The management organizations of the places of religious activity shall obtain a Place of Religious Activity Annual Inspection Form from the departments

112

responsible for the annual inspection and fill it in according to the requirements set out in the Notice of Annual Inspection. The completed forms shall be returned to the departments responsible for the annual inspection after comments have been entered and signed by the Township People's Governments or the urban Street Committee Offices.

Article 7: The departments responsible for the annual inspection shall examine the management situation in the places of religious activity and enter and sign their comments on the Place of Religious Activity Annual Inspection Forms in accordance with the Management of Places of Religious Activity Ordinance and the Method of Registration for Places of Religious Activity, as well as the relevant stipulations of other laws, regulations and policies.

Article 8: The annual inspection evaluation is either "pass" or "fail."

Article 9: Places of religious activity which fulfill the following requirements shall be classified as having passed the annual inspection:
a. Obeying the law, regulations and relevant policy regulations;
b. Not conducting any religious or foreign-related activity which is illegal or against the rules;
c. Conducting activities in accordance with all the rules and regulations in existence at the place of religious activity;
d. The financial system is in good shape and the income and expenditures are in accordance with relevant national regulations;
e. Having proceeded on time with the formalities of putting on record any changes in registration and establishments.
f. Operating seriously in accordance with democratic procedures;
g. Accepting annual inspection within the specified time limit.

Article 10: Places of religious activity involved in any one of the following situations shall be classified as having failed the annual inspection:
a. Breaking the law, regulations or relevant policy regulations;
b. Conducting religious or foreign-related activity which is illegal or against the rules;
c. Conducting activity which is not in accordance with the rules and regulations in existence at the place of religious activity.
d. Breaking the relevant financial regulations;
e. Not having gone through the formalities of putting on record any changes in registration and establishments;

f. Important activities lacking democratic procedures;
g. Not accepting annual inspection within the specified time limit without reasonable excuse;
h. Falsification in the annual inspection;
i. Breaking other relevant regulations.

Article 11: Places of religious activity which pass the annual inspection shall have their Place of Religious Activity Inspection Certificates stamped with the annual inspection stamp by the departments responsible for the annual inspection.

Article 12: Places of religious activity which fail the annual inspection shall receive a written explanation from the departments responsible for the annual inspection and shall be given a time limit to rectify the situation.

Article 13: Those places that rectify their situation within the given time shall have their Place of Religious Activity Inspection Certificates stamped with the annual inspection stamp by the departments responsible for the annual inspection.

Article 14: Regarding any place that does not accept annual inspection, fails to rectify its situation within the given time, or breaks the law, the department responsible for the annual inspection may ask the responsible person of the place's management organization to take responsibility for the matter, and, according to the seriousness of the situation, punish the place by issuing a warning to the place, ordering it to cease its activities or canceling its registration. Where the situation is especially serious, the department may ask the People's Government at (the appropriate) level to close down the place in accordance with the law.

Article 15: If the management organization of a place of religious activity disagrees with the administrative decision concerning it made by the department responsible for the annual inspection, it may apply for reconsideration or make an administrative appeal in accordance with the stipulations of the relevant laws and regulations.

Article 16: The departments responsible for the annual inspection shall forward the results of the annual inspection to the Religious Affairs Departments at the next higher level for the record. The Religious Affairs Departments at provincial level should make a general report on the provinces' annual inspection to the State Council Religious Affairs Bureau.

Article 17: The Place of Religious Activity Annual Inspection Form and the Place of Religious Activity Inspection Certificate shall be printed by the Provincial, Autonomous Regional or Municipal Government religious affairs departments in accordance with the design set out by the State Council Religious Affairs Bureau.

Article 18: Provincial, Autonomous Regional or Municipal Government religious affairs departments may, in accordance with the Method, set out suggestions as to its implementation according to actual local conditions. These shall be reported to the State Council Religious Affairs Bureau for the record.

Article 19: The State Council Religious Affairs Bureau shall supervise the implementation of this Method.

Article 20: The responsibility for interpreting this Method lies with the State Council Religious Affairs Bureau.

Article 21: The Method enters into force on the day of promulgation (July 29, 1996).

Religious Affairs Bureau State Council
July 29, 1996

(Translation by UCANews, January 13, 1997.)

APPENDIX X: CHINA'S CURRENT RELIGIOUS QUESTION: ONCE AGAIN AN INQUIRY INTO THE FIVE CHARACTERISTICS OF RELIGION

(March 22, 1996)
by Ye Xiaowen, Director, Bureau of Religious Affairs, the State Council

From "Selection of Reports of the Party School of the Central Committee of the Chinese Communist Party, 1996, No.5
This restricted circulation issue must be carefully kept and must not be reprinted without permission.

Religion is a complex social phenomenon. There are different definitions of religion. The religious question is a complicated one. Marx said: "Religion is Weltanschauung standing on its head. Religion is the general theory about this world, its all-embracing program, its popular logic." Where then shall we start talking about the religious question?

In today's world, with bipolar confrontation evolving into multipolarity, national contradictions and religious disputes are becoming prominent; they frequently lead to bloody conflicts and local wars, making the world unsafe. Many foreign scholars believe that in the twenty-first century, the religious question will be a prominent one in the world. Where then shall we begin talking about the current religious question?

Our country is in an important stage, with reform and opening to the outside world in our modernization efforts carrying on the past and opening a way for the future, and with the economic system in transition and increasing exchanges with foreign countries, new and old ideas clash and right or wrong become blurred. How shall we treat our traditional culture (which of course includes our religious culture), carrying forward the good and discarding the bad? How shall we treat foreign culture (which of course includes world religious culture), accepting the beneficial and resisting the harmful? How shall we deal with ideas arising from the market economy (which to be sure includes religious ideas that depend on and are adapted to a certain social economic system, such as those expounded by Max Weber in his *The Protestant Ethic and the Spirit of Capitalism*), promoting the positive and resisting the negative? How are we in this to shape values, the way of thinking, and the environment of opinion that bear Chinese characteristics, and are beneficial to reform and opening and the construction of socialist modernization? This is a complicated task that requires correct guidance and careful handling. This gigantic, complex work naturally includes the correct treatment and careful handling of China's religious question. So where do we start talking about our country's religious question?

116

To talk about "our current religious question" is to talk about that "all-embracing program." Where indeed shall we start talking about the outstanding question in the twenty-first century, about the most profound transformation in the transforming world?

We can choose different angles and make different summaries. In my opinion, a better angle and better summary would be to start with the five characteristics of religion.

The five characteristics of religion (i.e., the long-term character, the mass character, the national character, the international character, and the complex character of religion) represent the Chinese communists' scientific theoretical concept derived from realistic observation of religions in China and applying the Marxist view of religion to China's religious question.

Origin of the Theory of Five Characteristics of Religion
Everyone who deals with the nationalities and religion knows about a well-known survey, the sweeping survey of the state of implementation of the nationalities policy throughout China in the early fifties. Everyone knows about a famous report, *Summary of the Main Experience of the Party in Working in the National Minorities Areas in the Last Few Years,* drafted by the United Front Work Department of the Central Committee headed by Comrade Li Weihan, discussed by the Politburo and highly praised by Chairman Mao. In that report, there is a well-known formulation: "certain comrades in certain areas committed the error of impetuosity and rash advance precisely because they failed to understand the above-mentioned long-term character, national character, and international character of the religions of the national minorities...What they did not only failed to eradicate or weaken the religions, on the contrary, strengthened the minorities' religious belief because they felt their religious feelings were suppressed." That formulation was in fact the theory of the five characteristics of religion in its embryonic form. Later, in 1958, the five characteristics of religion were formulated at the Fifth National Conference on the Work on Religion. At the Sixth National Conference on the Work on Religion held in 1960, Comrade Zhang Zhiyi, former deputy director of the Central Committee's Department of United Front Work, expounded the five characteristics of religion. In 1981, the year of setting wrong things right, Mr. Zhao Puchu wrote an article summarizing the five characteristics as "the several objectively existing basic social characteristics of

religion."[160] By 1989, Comrade Jiang Ping, former deputy director of the Central Committee's Department of United Front Work, published a special article "The Origin and Practical Significance of the Five Characteristics of Religion."[161] They all stressed the significance of this theory as a guide to action.

In the opinion of some scholars, all ideologies have those five characteristics, and they are not unique to religion, and it is not necessary to talk about the five characteristics when talking about religion. As I see it, the five characteristics of religion have their specific connotation. To be sure, they should be assigned specific connotation in the light of actual conditions.

The Long-term Character
l. Religion will exist over a long period of time throughout the socialist period.

Religion goes through the process of emergence, development, and extinction. It will exist over a long period of time throughout the period of socialism. We cannot eradicate religion by administrative power; nor can we develop religion by the use of administrative power.

Because China's party in power is guided by the scientific world view of dialectical materialism and historical materialism (which includes atheism) and because of the antagonism between the two world views of materialism and idealism (which includes theism), some of our comrades cannot tolerate "unorthodox ideologies" that should be tolerated. They are unable to seek common ground while reserving differences. Some of them would not even have breakfast until the enemy is wiped out. They will not be happy until religion is eradicated at the earliest possible time. The Central Committee had criticized this view and action in two passages since the founding of the People's Republic. These passages need to be recalled.

The first passage is from the famous report on the general inspection of policies of 1953, dealing with the long-term character of religion. It reads:"Communists are atheists and materialists. They are not religious believers. But the way the Communist Party tries to dissuade the working people from believing in religion is not by intervening by administrative order, but mainly by

---

[160] See "Understanding of Certain Theoretical and Practical Problems in Religion," in *Theoretical Trends (Lilundongtai)*, Party School of the Central Committee of the Chinese Communist Party, 1981, No. 254.

[161] Jiang Ping, *Collections of Essays on Nationalities and Religion*, Publishing House of the History of the Communist Party.

political, economic, cultural, and educational development, and by the practice of social reform, naturally, indirectly, and in a roundabout way, gradually to weaken the influence of religion. Any simple and impetuous way would be erroneous. As Lenin taught: "This struggle must be linked with the actual practice of the class movement to eradicate the social basis of religion." Lenin severely criticized the attempts to "overthrow religion" by atheistic propaganda as "a superficial, bourgeois, and narrow culturalist concept. This is because "fear creates God." It is the expression of mankind in the face of natural and social forces that it cannot understand and considers irresistible. And so it seeks help from a mythical force. That was why primitive religious concepts arose in the primitive society. It became systematic religion in the class societies. It grew rapidly as the exploiting classes used it as an instrument to serve their own interests. Since religion arose and developed in this way, its eradication is possible only when mankind has eliminated classes and when it has vastly enhanced its power to control the forces of nature."

The other passage is from Document No. 19 of the Central Committee of 1982 entitled "Basic Concept and Basic Policy Concerning the Religious Question in China's Socialist Period." It further analyzed why religion would survive over a long period of time throughout the socialist period. It pointed out that in socialist society, "as a result of the fact that human consciousness always lags behind its social existence, the old ideas and old habits left over from the old society cannot be thoroughly eradicated in a short period of time. It requires a prolonged period of arduous struggle to achieve a very high level of the productive forces, a superabundance of material wealth, and a high degree of socialist democracy, as well as highly developed education, culture, science, and technology. And as mankind is not free from all kinds of hardships resulting from natural and man-made disasters; and as the class struggle goes on within certain areas and we live in a complex international environment, religion would inevitably hold sway over some people in the socialist society over a long period of time....The idea that religion will rapidly wither away with the establishment of the socialist system and a certain degree of economic and cultural development is unrealistic. The idea and practice that religion can be eradicated at one stroke by administrative order or other coercive means run counter to the basic Marxist concept of religion and are totally erroneous and harmful."

One of these two passages was addressed to "the error of impetuosity and rapid advance" with regard to religion committed in the early years of the People's Republic (of China). The other was addressed to the error of using force against religion during the Cultural Revolution. There are lessons clearly defined. Today, we certainly will not again commit the errors of "impetuosity and rapid advance" or the "use of force." But these are years when religion is rather hot. Indeed, we can even say this has been the most active period since the founding of the People's Republic. We need to calm down and relearn these passages and throw some cold water on ourselves. It does not mean we should allow the religious fever to rise freely. It means we need to coolly observe, prudently handle, carefully think through, and find a good policy.

2. The long-term character involves stages, zigzags, and relapses.

By the long-term character we mean that the development of religion itself is a prolonged process. Our handling of the religious question and the successful performance of our work on religion are correspondingly also a process. Haste and impatience will not do. Nor can we afford to relax. The long-term character necessarily means a process and stages. The fact that we cannot eradicate religion by administrative order does not mean we like religion and would try to promote its growth by administrative means. Even though we will do it naturally, indirectly, and in a roundabout way, we will gradually weaken the influence of religion. In the last decade and more, however, the influence of religion has not been weakened; instead it has grown greatly. How did that happen? As I see it, the phenomenon has to be analyzed in view of the long-term character of religion, which involves stages, zigzags, and relapses as well as generalities and particularities.

There are general causes why religion has grown in the past decade and more, i.e., the existence of old ideas, the backwardness of the productive forces, the scarcity of material wealth, natural and manmade disasters, the class struggle, and the international environment — factors pointed out in document No. 19. There are also particular causes.

• Looking at the social background, the development and energizing of religion often accompanied great social changes and transformations. According to statistics compiled by the Center of Religious Research, the number of religious believers in the Russian Federal Republic made up 22 percent of the population before the disintegration of the Soviet Union. By 1994, it had risen to 50 percent. In the Republic of Korea, Catholics and Protestant Christians constituted 7 percent of the population in 1947. It rose to 21 percent by 1985. Ordinarily one would expect the development of religion to be in inverse proportion to the degree of economic development. But this was not so in the past several decades in the ROK and some other countries. Conditions in our country differ from those in Russia and the ROK. But China is also going through a period of profound change in the economic system and social life. Contradictions intertwine and benefits and maladies go hand in hand. It is possible for all kinds of religions to find the necessary conditions for their existence and growth. With the development of the market economy, many people come under the sway of the spontaneous play of the law of value. They try to get rich with the secret help of divinities to the point that even "six" [*shun,* meaning success] and "eight" [*fa*, meaning get rich] have become deified lucky numbers. This has provided the solid social psychological basis for the development of religion. And with the increasing openness to the outside world, influence and infiltration by foreign religious forces have also increased.

- Looking at our work. There is reaction to the ultra-left of the Cultural Revolution. Having restored the freedom of religious belief, the management of religious affairs according to law has lagged. Especially at the grassroots level, our work has been weak and demoralized. There is the problem of "one hand hard and one hand soft" in our practical work. Our control of the rural society has weakened. The burden imposed on the peasantry has become more onerous. And the gap between rich and poor has widened. The lack of medical insurance and the worsening of public security, all provided the objective conditions for the development of religion. There is a "crisis of faith" among some cadres and popular masses whose faith in Marxism-Leninism and Mao Zedong Thought has been shaken. In addition, the traditional ideological and political work sound preachy, without adequate consideration of the harmonizing of human relations and the adjustment of social psychology. Insufficient attention has been paid to the psychological changes of the ordinary people and insufficient solicitude has been shown their psychological needs in a period of social transformation. It is precisely in these respects that religion has appealed to a large number of people. Some local governments put forth the slogan, "Religion sets the stage for the economy to perform." Some leading cadres even personally participate in religious activities. That helps increase the religious fever. The disorganization of grassroots rural political power has made it possible for the emergence and spread of cults in certain areas.

- Looking at religion itself. Religion is a dynamic social phenomenon. China has entered a period in which religions safely exist and are ready for powerful growth. Religion has gone through three stages since the founding of the People's Republic: before the Cultural Revolution, religion was in the stage of shaking itself free from colonial and feudal characteristics. It was too occupied to develop. During the Cultural

Revolution, religion was basically in a stage of persecution and suppression. It was too weak to grow. Since 1982, with the adjustment and earnest implementation of the policy toward religion, the latter has been assured legitimate existence. Conditions for normal activities have been provided and some growth has been inevitable. Buddhism, Daoism and Islam, which have a long historical tradition in China, possess their own impulse to recover, expand, and increase their influence. Protestant and Catholic Christianity, which came to China relatively late, have gone through a long period of adjustment and gradually adapted themselves to Chinese culture. Its missionary model has also been sinicized in some ways. These are all factors by which the religions can promote themselves at the present time.

The religious fever of the third stage (not only has religion developed relatively rapidly, many disorderly phenomena have emerged) was in fact a reaction against the suppression of religion during the second stage. As a young scholar has pointed out, "The bogus deification of social culture (it was in fact idolatry) and the bogus orderliness (it was in fact unitary readjustment) have accumulated the power to turn themselves into their opposite, i.e., excessive secularization (it was in fact worship of material things) and disorderliness (it was in fact cynicism)."[162]
We need to analyze the development of religion and its growing influence soberly and deal with it seriously. We need to recognize that the religious circle is on the whole stable and law-and-discipline-abiding. Exaggeration of the seriousness of the existing problems and becoming panic-stricken, or being blind to those problems and treating them lightly do not accord with the actual situation and will not help us in our work.

3.There is a positive side to the long-term character.
When we talk about the long-term character of religion, we are generally talking about the gradual and prolonged process of religion naturally withering away, and the possibility and zigzag nature of religion rebounding during a certain historical stage. All this is talking about religion from a negative angle. As a matter of fact, everything represents a dialectical unity. There are both a negative and a positive side to the long-term character of religion. It is precisely in the long-term character of Chinese religion that there resides the fine tradition of thousands of

---

[162] Notes are taken from He Guanghu, "Outline Theory on the Reform of Religion in China," The East (Dongfang), 1995, No.1.

years without interruption of love of the country and love for the church and unity for progress — a tradition that needs to be carried forward. Love of country and love of church is not unique to China. But a tradition of thousands of years without interruption is rarely seen elsewhere in the world.

There are great differences between the history of development of the Chinese nation, the history of development of Chinese religions, and the history of development of the West and Western religions. The Chinese nation has the longest history and the richest cultural heritage and a fine national tradition that has never been interrupted. Let us look at the cultural development of the four great states of ancient civilization in the world, Egypt, ancient Babylon, China, and India, and the origin and development of the three great world religions, Buddhism, Christianity (including the Roman Catholic Church, the Orthodox Church, and the Protestant Churches). In this long history of cultural development, in which economic growth, class struggle, systemic changes, and succession of states took place, China is the only country among the four great states of ancient civilization in which generation has succeeded generation; the main body of the country's civilization has never been interrupted by a foreign civilization. As early as 219 B.C., China was unified by the First Emperor of Qin who introduced the unified wheel base for chariots, a unified written language, unified weights and measures, abolished divided fiefdoms, and established the system of prefectures and counties. The Han dynasty carried forward the Qin institutions, and so the Chinese became known as the "Han" people. The cultural tradition was handed down generation after generation. During the Yuan and Qing dynasties, the minority nationalities became masters of the Central Plains.But that did not represent replacement of one culture by another. Rather, it was a fusion of national cultures. Thus, in the history of the world viewed as a long process of thousands of years, "love of country" and "love of the church" in other countries and among believers of other nations were often interrupted from time to time as a result of historical change. Whereas in China, Chinese religious believers have been fused in one over thousands of years without interruption. Those religions that came to China from abroad, including the so-called foreign religions, can find a footing and develop only by respecting and adapting themselves to the Chinese tradition of patriotism. The Chinese nation has never been exclusively Han, but has always included minority nationalities. Members of the big family of the Chinese nation have never been exclusively atheists; theists have always been included. China has never been a nation only of the Han people. It has always been a nation of the Han and minority peoples (including those minorities virtually all members of which believe in a certain religion). The rise of the Chinese nation today means the rise of all fifty-six nationalities. Han and the minorities cannot live without each other. Patriotism is the common national trait.

Over the ages, many patriots, including patriotic religious leaders, have regarded national integrity as the highest virtue, even more precious than life itself. Using the past as a mirror we come to a better understanding of the present. Since religion will exist over a long period of time throughout the socialist society and we will have to live with religion for a long time, and since there is the historical tradition of the unity of love of country and love of church, why wouldn't we observe the objective law, bring the advantage of our tradition into play, and work hard to guide the religious believers to better combine love of church with love of country? When dealing with our work on religion in his report to the Fourth Session of the Eighth National People's Congress, Premier Li Peng added the phrase "We should educate religious believers in love of country and love of church" to his finalized version at the suggestion of the delegates. Well done!

4. The root causes of the long-term character are poverty and benightedness.

The long-term character of China's religious question arises to a very great extent from the difficulty in solving the problem of poverty and in building the two civilizations in the rural areas. Poverty gives rise to a desire for change. If one cannot get rich in this life, one dreams of getting rich in the next life. Marx said, "The hardship in religion is an expression of the hardship in real life; it is also a protest against that hardship. Religion is the sigh of the oppressed soul, the feeling of a heartless world, just like it is the spirit of a spiritless system. Religion is the people's opium."[163] The poor also want a spiritual life. Some rituals of religion powerfully attract those peasants who live in out-of-the-way villages and have no cultural life to talk about. The poor are more sympathetic. The "love"advertised by religion calls on them to be converted. The poor are mortally

---

[163] Qian Zhongshu in his *On Guan Zhui*, did textual research into Marx's famous thesis that "religion is the opium of the people." His work helps deepen our understanding: "Marx describes religion as people's protest against the reality of hardship, just like the opium of the people." Novalis, the romantic poet, said long ago that the Philistines' belief in religion to quell their sorrows and sufferings was only as effective as smoking opium. He also said that all common people smoke spiritual opium and intoxicate themselves in false belief. Later, some novelists described those who did not believe in Christianity as not seeking remedy from opium. Some philosophers likened religion to taking a narcotic to kill toothache. Marx's thesis is the sharpest and most direct. Heinrich Heine, on many occasions, used that metaphor. For example, in remembering his dead friend he called religion "a tasty hypnotic liquid, the spiritual opium." Again in a letter from Paris in 1840, he talked about Englishmen becoming more and more decadent, just like the Chinese who shun the military. "Religious piety he had pietism is the opium," that is most at fault.

afraid of sickness. The poor and sick have nowhere to go, except to plead with God "to cure the sickness and chase away the devil." So in some rural areas "curing the sickness and chasing away the devil" has been an important reason why peasants have been converted into religious believers. Those areas interest the missionaries most. Certain foreign Christian organizations have devised one hundred methods for missionaries to proselytize in the rocky mountains of Guangxi province. To be sure, we also want to work in those areas. But to work there we need funding. It is true "work on religion is never trivial"; it is always important. But we cannot carry on our work with neither large nor small funding. As our economy is backward, our opinion carries little weight. As the popular masses put it, you cannot carry out the spirit of the meeting merely by holding meetings; neither can you carry out the spirit of the document merely by issuing the document; nor can you carry out the spirit of the speech merely by making speeches.

The Mass Character
1. It is an objective fact that the number of believers is very large. We need to keep these people in mind.

How large really is the number of Chinese religious believers? It is very difficult to count. Why? There is no objective criteria. There are rough numbers of those who have been baptized or initiated into monkhood or nunhood. It is difficult to count the number of those who have not been initiated but are believers. There is also a subjective factor. There is a saying, "The cadres produce the figures, and the figures make the cadres." (More precisely concerning the religious question: "The cadres produce the negative figures, and the negative figures make the cadres.") So in the case of the number of religious believers, we can only use statistics plus estimates. A more authoritative estimate puts the number of Chinese religious believers at several tens of millions, a figure used by the late Premier Zhou and still being used today. That figure, combined with those who worship at home, amounts to roughly 100 million. Based on that estimate, the present number would be more than 100 million.

When we talk about the mass character of religion, we should recognize that there is a large number, some 100 million religious believers. Nevertheless, they remain our basic masses. Or put it another way, precisely because these 100 million people are our basic masses and constitute a very large number, we need to respect their religious belief and their religious feeling. And we should try to meet the needs of their religious life. As some veteran comrades recall, Premier Zhou once remarked, "We must understand that even if we will not show respect for the monk, we must show respect for Buddha." By "Buddha," he was actually talking about the masses. We must not regard these 100 million people as an alien force, and "drive the fish into deep water and the sparrows into the thickets." Instead we should treat them as an important force in the building of socialist modernization, as important as the rest of the masses — 1.1 billion of them. We must not overlook the fact that believers and non-believers share the same fundamental political and economic interests even though they have different faiths. The policy of freedom of religious belief is a policy for uniting the broad masses of believers to build our great country together with the non-believers. It is a policy that is truly in the fundamental interest of the 100 million people, and also in the common interest of the 1.2 billion people. Fulfilment of the Ninth Five-Year Plan and the long-range targets set for 2010 is a process in which the Chinese people creates history under the leadership of the Chinese Communist Party. In that process, the 100 million believers also play a leading role. They should be allowed to play their historical role fully, and no one else can substitute for them.

Religion has a broad influence among compatriots in Taiwan, Hong Kong, and Macao as well as among overseas Chinese. Successful work on religion will help us win over and unite with them. It also plays a very significant role in our efforts to recover Hong Kong and Macao and maintain prolonged stability and prosperity there in accordance with the principle of "one country two systems," and to promote the return of Taiwan to the embrace of the motherland, thus bringing to a conclusion the great cause of unification.

2. The correct approach to the religious question also means adopting a correct attitude toward the masses.

Talking about the mass character of religion means that the correct handling of the religious question is also a question of adopting a correct attitude toward the masses. Work on religion is also mass work. The communist party thrives on the masses. Everything the party does is for the greatest majority of the masses. The party's special skill is in mass work. The support of the masses is our greatest advantage. Divorce from the masses and we have nothing and nothing can be accomplished. Let us assume the extreme: if for whatever reason a large number of people, say 100 million religious believers turn against us, we will be at the end of our tether and we will not have a single day of tranquility.

As far as the religious question is concerned, when contradictions become sustained and large-scale and emerge in the form of irrepressible mass antagonism, it would not do simply to blame it on "the scheme of a very few evil elements." There is no harm in asking the question: why is it that "a very few" can control the vast majority. Our mission is to "work for the well-being of the great majority." Why then in this case have we lost the great majority? It is necessary promptly to mete out punishment to the evil elements. To be sure, temporary lack of awareness on the part of the masses could be another factor. But if we err in our work, we should not exaggerate the role of the evil elements, or use the backwardness of the masses as an excuse to cover up our own error. Whether we are good at mass work, especially at mass work winning over those religious believers who were hoodwinked for the moment, reflects the level of our art of leadership, the effectiveness of our mass work.

3. When we talk about the mass character, we don't mean that we should accommodate ourselves to the backwardness of the masses. But we should be good at working with the backward masses.

When we talk about the mass character of religion, we don't mean that we should accommodate ourselves to the backwardness of the masses, still less do we mean that we should tolerate a minority who damage the interests of the majority and destabilize the overall situation. Those who refuse to give heed to exhortations, who refuse to be reasonable, and who persist in illegal activities in the name of religion are to be promptly curbed according to law. Upholding the dignity of law is consistent with safeguarding the interests of the people. Persistent quarrels between different religious sects in Zheherenye in Xiji county, the Ningxia Hui Autonomous Region, led to large scale fighting with weapons. Forty-nine people were killed within a single year. We are of the opinion that disputes between the sects could have been patiently mediated. Just as with quarrels between husband and wife, the government could stay aloof without intervening. But when the dispute becomes so violent that one tries to kill the other, it damages the interest of the people and tramples on the dignity of the law. How can the government not intervene? In the case of the fighting between sects in Ningxia, we deployed a strong police force, disarmed them all, and resolutely stopped the fighting. We raised high two banners: safe-guarding the interests of the people, and defending the dignity of the law. The people welcome the force of justice. In a certain sense, work on religion is mass work, a rather special kind of mass work. We need to enhance our competence in working with this portion of the masses through practical work and raise the level of our work. And we need to be extremely prudent in handling matters that involve religious believers and try to avoid those improper measures that would push the majority of the people to the opposite side, thus artificially creating enemies and asking for trouble. It could be counterproductive to try to contain the growth of religion simply by administrative means; that could accelerate its growth. Comrade (Deng) Xiaoping said: "It will not do to deal with religion and administrative order. On the other hand, religion should not go so far as to become fanatical. That would be against socialism and the interests of the people." If we give it a free hand and allow it to drift, it will become overheated, even to the point of fanaticism. We must raise high the banner of "patriotism and love of the church and unity for progress," firmly uphold the principles of safeguarding the interests of the people, defending the dignity of the law, defending national unity, and defending the unification of the motherland, and stop religion from becoming fanatical or turning into fanaticism (go back one). However, in handling the religious question we must not go to the extreme or become too impatient, unless we were absolutely forced to do so. Otherwise, it could easily touch off an explosive crisis, turning a potential danger into a real one. Our experience of many years has proved that the religious question which involves the masses is easily tied into a knot that is very difficult to untie. So it is better to untie it and avoid tying it. It is also easy to come together and difficult to scatter. So it is better to scatter it and avoid it coming together. It is easy to become blocked and difficult to dredge. So it is better to dredge it than block it up. In handling individual religious cases we must do everything possible to pull it out of the category of a religious question and handle it from the legal angle so as to avoid a frontal clash with religion.

The National Character
1. We must be good at understanding the difference between the religious and the national questions and the link between them.

When we talk about the national character of religion, we must first recognize that the religious question is, to a very great extent, linked with the national question. We must be good at understanding the difference between the religious and the national questions as well as the link between them and handle them correctly. Religion and nationalism are two different categories. Religion has never been a prerequisite for the formation of a nation, nor does it constitute a basic characteristic of a nation. The two should not be mixed up. However, in our country, a multinational socialist country, the religious question is often closely linked with the national question. The Tibetan sect of Buddhism, the Southern sect of Buddhism, and Islam have large and pious followings among different minorities in China. They are the majority religions among some twenty minority groups. Some are even the religions of entire minority groups. The Tibetan sect of Buddhism has followings among the Tibetans, Mongolians, Tus, Qiangs, Pumis, Nus, and Yugus, etc. The Southern sect of Buddhism has followings among the Thais, Achangs, Deangs, Was, and Bulangs. Adherents of Islam are the Huis, Uighurs, Kazakhs, Dongxiangs, Salas, Kirgizs, Tajiks, Uzbeks, Tartars, and Baoans, etc. Among these minorities, religion and the nation share four major common traits, common language, common geographical area, common economic life, and common psychological quality, as an expressions of common national cultural characteristics; the two are closely bound up. In the world at large, any world religion can thrive only by fusing itself with a particular national culture, i.e., through the process of "indigenization." And once a religion takes root in a certain nation, it exerts a great influence over the development of that nation. In a nation with a broad-based and profound religious belief, the religious and national sentiments, the religious and national psychology, the religious and national customs, the religious and national culture, and the religious and national consciousness of every believer are intertwined and infiltrate each other, sometimes even becoming inseparable. So we come to understand why the question of pork eating is such a sensitive issue among the broad masses of the Moslems. And so also we come to understand why we ask those communists who live among minority nationalities where virtually everyone of them is a religious believer, especially those who work at the grassroots level, to keep in touch with the masses. In order to do so, they must draw an ideological demarcation line with religious belief on the one hand. On the other, they must respect and go along with the customs and habits of the minorities that bear some religious color and tradition. They must not become believers themselves. But they may take part in wedding and funeral ceremonies and mass activities that bear some religious color and tradition.

We must be good at understanding the link between the religious and national questions. At the same time, we must also recognize the differences between the two. After all, we cannot regard religion and nation as one and the same thing. If we accommodate ourselves totally with the views of the religious believers, and regard all religious sentiments, psychology, customs and habits, and culture as identical with national sentiments, psychology, customs and habits and culture, and therefore absolutely untouchable, we would be moving from the view of the supremacy of religion to narrow nationalism that hinders the development and progress of that nation. In fact, even during the Middle Ages in the West, when religious culture ruled everywhere, the heliocentric theory, a product of the scientific culture opposed to the religious culture, was developed by national progressive elements. Today, when we handle the religious question, we need to keep our eyes on the fundamental interests of the nation, its long-term development and progress, rely on the initiative of the advanced elements of that nation, base our judgement on the wishes of the great majority of that nation, and gradually change those customs and habits that are harmful to the production, life and physical and mental health of the masses, as well as those canon laws, corrupt customs, and religious institutions that hinder the development and progress of that nation.

2. The peculiar two-fold role of religion on the minority nationalities.

When we talk about the national character of religion, we need to recognize the peculiar two-fold role of religion on the minority nationalities. As Comrade Li Weihan pointed out in his article "Outline on the Question of the Hui Nationality" published as early as 1940, when there is national oppression, on the one hand, religion plays the role of a sacred banner under which the national fights national oppression and serves as important tie for national unity. On the other hand, religion becomes an obstacle to the cultural development and national awakening and class consciousness of that nation. It is used by the dark forces both within and outside that nation as an instrument to consolidate their position. That two-fold role may be summed up as a sacred banner and used by the dark forces. How then is this two-fold role demonstrated today? To be sure, we should not look at it as in the period of national oppression. But religion exists and nationalities exits. The role of religion on the nationalities can still be analyzed from those two angles. Let us first look at it as a sacred banner. The mission of fighting national oppression is a thing of the past, because there is no more national oppression. It is obviously out of date and no longer necessary to use religion to unite with and mobilize people, as we have already established a new socialist relationship between the nationalities, a relationship of equality, unity and mutual help. But religion still has the power to unite and mobilize among the national minorities. This makes it necessary for us to provide guidance in a very prudent way. This is because there are still differences and contradictions among the nationalities. On the basis of common fundamental interests, there are still contradiction in the form of differences in the specific interests between different groups of the masses, and between the popular masses and the state. The gap between the rich and the poor and between different areas may grow as a result of uneven development. It is unavoidable that these contradictions will find expression in national sentiments and consciousness. Religion is still a sacred banner with mobilizing power among some minority nationalities. If these national sentiments and consciousness and discontent are enlarged to welcome antagonism, it may evolve into nationalities questions hard to handle. To "unite and struggle" under this banner, but against whom? It can only sadden one's own people and gladden the enemy. Let us now look at the use of religion by the dark forces. In recent years, we have seen how certain forces and individuals belonging to certain sects frequently used religion to scramble for power and profit, and stir up trouble, even to the point of hurting the people. Interference in the executive, the judicial, the educational and nuptial affairs as well as meddling in the production and life of the masses by the use of religion happen from time to time. In certain places, things have gone so far as the restoration of the religious feudal privileges and corrupt customs that have long been abolished. What is especially worthy of our vigilance is that hostile international forces are brazenly supporting the national splittist forces in our country. They are using the national and religious questions to find a break through point, and are intensifying their infiltration, sabotage, splittist and subversive activities. The national splittist elements in China, acting as their planted agents, are using religious fanaticism to divide the people, undermine the unification of the motherland and the unity of the various nationalities. Our struggle against the splittist Dalai clique over the Tibetan question is in essence not a matter of whether there should be religious belief or whether there should be autonomy, but whether there should be stability or disorder in Tibet; a matter of safeguarding the unification or dividing the motherland, of upholding the dignity of national sovereignty or interfering in China's internal affairs in collusion with hostile foreign forces. The Xinjiang question is not so prominent as the Tibetan one. But the potential problem calls for our attention. The major danger affecting the stability of Xinjiang, especially southern Xinjiang, comes primarily from national splittism. The danger, in addition to direct sabotage, lies in their ability to use the growing national and religious sentiments and estrangement to cover themselves and avoid punishment, their ability to use errors in our work to sow dissension and stir up trouble, their ability to use the ideological trend of pan-Islamism and pan-Turkism to develop themselves. In a word, it is easy for them to hide behind the contradictions among the people. so that when we try to fight them, people are likely to have different opinions and measures are difficult to implement. The targets are obscured which makes it hard to strike at. We need to conduct in-depth research, consider all relevant factors and suit the remedy to the case. Implementation must be firm. If we do not think about the long-term danger, we will have immediate problems. In history, the Qing dynasty brought about border peace through the correct handling of the religious question. In this, they exerted a great effort. We should be much more competent than the Qing government.

The International Character
1. Religion is an international phenomenon

We talk about the international character of religion because first of all religion is an international phenomenon. There is not a single country in the world without a religion, Christianity, Islam and Buddhism are world religions. According to the *Great Britain Statistical Year Book of 1990*, world population reached 5.2 billion by 1989, and the believers of various religions numbered 4.1 billion or 78.8 percent of the total population. Of these Christians numbered 1.712 billion, or 41.75 percent of all the believers; Moslems numbered over 900 million, 22.56 percent of all believers; Buddhists numbered over 300 million, or 7.59

percent of all believers; followers of other religions such as Hinduism, Judaism, Shintoism and Bahaism and other regional religions total over one billion, or 28.01 percent of the world's believers. in Asia, Buddhism and Islam have broad social influence. The influence of religions penetrate the political, economic and cultural spheres. Some are designated state religions.

2. Consider religion from the height of overall world development.

Speaking of the international character of religion, we need to consider the religious question from the height of overall world development, and always pay attention to international influence and world trends. In today's world, there are troubles in many places. The disintegration of the former Soviet Union, the conflicts in Bosnia-Herzegovina, the Middle East question, tribal conflicts in Mrica, etc. Most of these are nationality and religion related. There was once fierce fighting in Bosnia-Herzegovina. In addition to its international political background, the break up of the Roman Empire in the fourth century, the break up of Christianity of the eleventh century, both had their fault lines running through the Balkan Peninsula. History has foreshadowed later developments. At the turn of the century, the political role of religious crises is increasing in giving rise to social disturbances throughout the world, accelerating political change, causing ethnic conflicts, and creating splits in different countries. In China, the religious circles are stable. The contradictions in religion are primarily contradictions among the people and do not constitute a prominent social contradiction at the present time. But China is accelerating its opening and its march onto the world stage. The rapid development of science and technology is accelerating the spread of information throughout the world. It is hard to expect the "excitement" of religion throughout the world not to influence China in the long run. Internet is linking up the entire world. Information about the various religious questions is being spread rapidly along this information super highway that connects all parts of the world together. This has made it hard for us to pay attention to our own moral uplift without thought of others. Looking to the future, once the world enters the era of palm-size computers, some people will surely try to do missionary work by computer. The Government of Singapore recently decided to exercise strict control over the transmission of religious information through internet for the sake of national security, so as to prevent the transmission of pornography and materials that may give rise to religious or political disturbance. China has also demanded that owners of computers who use internet register with the authorities. But effective adrninistration remains to be worked out successfully and with foresight.

3. Resist infiltration under conditions of opening (to the outside world)

Speaking of the international character of religion, we need to study ways to develop normal and friendly international exchanges in the sphere of religion, while resolutely resisting infiltration in the new situation of expanded opening to the outside world. With the exception of Taoism, the other four religions now existing in China were introduced from abroad. And Taoism had been introduced to foreign countries. All five major religions in China have countless ties with foreign lands. With the increasing opening to the outside world, the religious circles also increase their outside ties. This plays a significant role in China increasing its political influence and promoting China's economic cooperation and cultural exchanges with foreign countries. But hostile international forces will use the nationalities and religions as the break through points in their efforts to "Westernize" and "divide" China. Reactionary international religious forces will also try their best to avail themselves of the opportunity to "return to mainland China" We must keep politics in mind. As a matter of fact, the bourgeois politicians are more politically minded as far as the religious question is concerned. Former U.S. Secretary of State Shultz said as early as more than a decade ago at the so-called conference on "the democratization of the communist countries" held in the United States, "it is only a small step from religious belief to political action." Their hope has always been that the Chinese religious believers would take that small step and take the "political action" that constantly destabilizes China. The Voice of America describes one of its missions as "stirring up religious fanaticism behind the Iron Curtain." In their research reports, the Institute of Strategic Studies of Harvard University and the Institute of International Affairs of Johns Hopkins University suggested that the United States use religion as its "weapon of first choice" to subvert China. The disintegration of the Soviet Union and the dramatic change in Eastern Europe resulted from their domestic political and economic failures and the sharpening of *social* contradictions there, including the failure of their policy toward religion over the long term that resulted in the alienation of the religious believers. Religion became a weapon in the hands of the dissidents for inciting the masses and creating political disturbances, thus hastening the collapse of the Soviet and Eastern European conununist parties. Today, with the support of the Vatican, the Catholic underground has few followers in China but considerable capabilities. It is still a serious test for us whether in the new situation of enlarged opening, the Christian church in China can keep operating successfully according to the "Three-Self Principle" without retrogression. A new feature of religious infiltration is luring the believers with profit, so many people simply flock to the church. Infiltration is inevitable as opening is enlarged. The various departments must coordinate their efforts and fight a prolonged general defensive war against infiltration by hostile foreign religious forces.

Since four-fifths of the world's population are religious believers, religion inevitably becomes a hot issue, and a country's attitude toward religion easily causes concern. "Religious intolerance" makes an embarrassing image in the world. China pursues a policy of freedom of religious belief and treats all religions on an equal basis. This is maximum religious tolerance. But the United States and other Western countries attack us often on the human rights issue and accuse us of "lack of protection for the freedom of religious belief." They maliciously slander us in world public opinion. In the realm of international human rights struggle, we must argue strongly on sound grounds, strengthen our foreign propaganda, and wage a prolonged struggle against the anti-China Western forces.

The Complex Character

I. Religion is a system with complex structures and functions

Religion itself is a complex system. It is made up of four basic elements, namely, sentiments (religious sentiments or experience); knowledge (religious concepts or ideas); conduct (religious conduct and activities); body (religious organizations and institutions). Sentiments and knowledge are the internal elements of religion, and are within the realm of ideological superstructure; they interact with the political and legal ideas, ethics, arts and philosophy of society to form a unique religious culture. Conduct and body are the external elements of religion, and are within the realm of social life; they are linked with the various aspects of society to form a special religious cause. They engage the various social organizations and entities and produce several religious affairs. Religious belief is the private business of a citizen, whereas religious organizations are social entities in public life. Religion is the fantasy of a person's circumstances, and that fantasy *is* inevitably complicated, conflising and variegated. The doctrines, canons, rituals and organizations of different religions form different systems and are unrelated. The different sects of the same religion are multifaceted and often incompatible. A scripture often has different and contradictory interpretations. An ocean collects a hundred rivers. A certain viewpoint often finds similar interpretations in different scriptures. and different views become one. Most religions seek truth, goodness and beauty, suppress the evil and extol the good and promote social harmony and stability. But religions have mass followings and directly relate to their sentiments and sub-consciousness. As a result of the sentiments affecting each other, identification with the same values, and behaviors stimulating each other, collective irrational fanaticism ensues. This contradictory expression of religion itself also conforms to the law of unity of opposites.

2. The characteristics of rehgious contradictions

In the above, we briefly described the complex structures and functions of religion. Precisely because of these structures and functions, even though the contradictions in China's religion are non-antagonisuc contradictions among the people, they are contradictions that can be sharpened easily, and the nature of the contradictions can easily be transformed. In my earlier articles, I described the five characteristics of these contradictions and the process of their cyclical change.

The first characteristic is accumulation. The contradictions among the people in religion are often the accumulation of all kinds of sentiments and opinions, the accumulation of all kinds of small frictions and small disputes, massive in quantity and very broad in coverage. The accumulation of quantity comes to a point when it leads to sudden qualitative change.

The second characteristic is sudden explosion. An accidental small matter, a single spark rapidly escalates because of lack of mutual accommodation. The contradiction could sharpen because of bureaucratic mishandling. Small matters soon become big ones, and big ones become disturbances because differences in opinion and matters that should have been reported to superior organs have not been reported, or when decisions should have been promptly made but not made in time, the opportunity was lost. The causes of trouble were accidental; but they necessarily led to trouble. Necessity always opens a way for itself through contingency.

The third is expansion. Religious belief, to a certain extent, has a special uniting and mobilizing power. It is especially sensitive and spreads very rapidly. Once an incident occurs, the self-preservation instinct in religious belief spreads rapidly and stirs up a fervor for resistance and a blind passion. The mass media in an information society help accelerate the process of this expansion.

The fourth is mutation. Non-antagonistic contradictions are transformed into antagonistic ones either because the nature of the contradictions changes, or the question of right or wrong is transformed into a question of the enemy and ourselves.

The fifth characteristic is precipitation. When the incident grows serious, persuasion and education no longer work and administrative measures have to be taken. The result is that superficially the contradiction seems to have been solved or relaxed. In fact, it has precipitated to a deeper level of the national or religious psyche. It becomes subconscious estrangement and accumulates in a way that is quietly making preparations for the contradiction to blow up again in the same or some other manner.

The five characteristics described above form a cyclical process as shown in the following diagram:

accumulation $\Rightarrow$ sudden explosion $\Rightarrow$ expansion$\Rightarrow$ mutation

$\Uparrow$

$\Leftarrow\Leftarrow\Leftarrow\Leftarrow\Leftarrow\Leftarrow\Leftarrow\Leftarrow\Leftarrow$ precipitation$\Leftarrow\Leftarrow\Leftarrow\Leftarrow\Leftarrow\Leftarrow\Leftarrow\Leftarrow$ $\Downarrow$

It is obvious that if we land ourselves in this predicament, it would be very difficult for us to solve the problem in its embryonic stage, at the grassroots level and among ourselves.

3. The complex expression of the link between religious and political questions

Also because of the characteristics of the complex structures and functions of religion, when the question of religious belief and the political question are linked together, this produces two diametrically opposed tendencies — cooperation and opposition. To be sure, we welcome the tendency of cooperation. It is our desire that the relationship between ourselves and the religious believers should be one of political unity and cooperation, and mutual respect for each other's faith." That kind of relationship is currently the main current in China and is being consolidated and developed. But the tendency of opposition is surety a headache. In that opposition, the secular "God" worshiped by the believers is at the same time the "devil" that leads the believers to oppose their state and split with their fellow countrymen, a political archenemy. "Man" is sandwiched between "God" and "devil" between the object of prostrate worship and the universally condemned arch-adversary. These are totally incompatible. Yet they are forced to become one in a certain religious belief. That unity as expressed in any individual believer inevitably leads to a dual personality derived from the two-fold character of belief, and that dual personality leads to schizophrenia. That unity as expressed in a collective religious organization inevitably leads to the dual character of that organization, which eventually evolves into an underground religious force. In dealing with religious belief, we must not use the method of administrative order But in handling the problem of political opposition, we must use administrative orders and even dictatorial measures. It is therefore an extremely complex job cracking down on the underground religious forces. We need to use administrative orders and even dictatorial measures. But these do not suffice. The best approach is to launch a psychological attack. That kind of attack vanquishes the opposition.

But it would be extremely difficult for us to launch a psychological attack without the help of the patriotic religious personages. This is because religious preaching goes on day after day after day; religious rituals are launching psychological attacks every day. Religious sentiments reject non-religious reason.

4. There are new species, sub-species, mutations, and bogus species of religions
The complexity of China's religious question today also finds expression in the fact that in addition to the five major religions — Catholicism, Protestantism, Buddhism, Taoism and Islam — that we recognize, there are all kinds of new species, sub-species, mutations and bogus species.

The first is newly emerging religion, new species of religion, imported from abroad. The First Amendment of the Constitution of the United States says that "all faiths public or privately held" may be considered religion and will be registered, protected and granted tax free status. As a result, newly emerging religions are very active in the United States and such countries as Korea and Japan under its influence. With the increase in our exchanges with foreign countries, certain newly emerging religions have also come into our country. They are characterized by "richness in funding, friendliness and missionary work" We need to investigate and study them before we decide on how to handle them.

The second is folk belief as a mutation of religion. How folk belief is to be defined; can it be regarded as a religion? There are many different views. In my opinion, the central idea of folk belief is about ghosts or gods, the soul or fate. It is a mixture of the traditional patriarchal and ancestral idea; the primitive, crude religious belief and ancestor worship plus folkways and customs, folk culture, superstition, as well as actual social and cultural life and social psychology. At the present time, folk beliefs are rather active in the coastal areas. We face an urgent task of investigation and study as to how to guide and manage them.

The third is cult, a mutation of religion. They are not religious organizations or sects, but heresies cooked up by a few rogue elements who have come together under the cloak of religion, and who quote fragments from religious scriptures and mix these with large amounts of feudal superstition to defraud the masses, set up secret societies to engage in unlawful criminal activities. These cults run rampant and grow rapidly and have become an evil force in certain rural areas, endangering social stability. These illegal organizations must be resolutely banned and eradicated according to law, and their illegal activities resolutely curbed. We must firmly crack down on those criminal elements according to law. But as far as these organizations are concerned, the question of religious belief is often intertwined with the political question, and the masses unaware of the truth are mixed with those evil elements with ulterior motives, non-antagonistic contradictions and antagonistic ones are mixed together, so when curbing illegal activities, we must strictly adhere to the demarcation line in policy, and educate and win over the deceived masses as much as possible, energetically strengthen the building of the four civilizations in the countryside, so as to maintain social stability.

The fourth is superstition. This is a bogus species of religion. Today, there are many shoddy, bogus, counterfeit goods. Superstition is also a bogus shoddy variety which looks like religion but actually is not. Although in a broad sense, religion is also superstition. But religion and superstition have their defining characteristics. We need to recognize the link between them. But we must not mix them together. If we draw a coordinate, its end point A is defined as a low, crude form of belief loosely and poorly organized, its means evil and despicable, specializing in falsehood, ugliness and evil doings, robbery and murder, playing the devil rather than playing god. The other end point of the coordinate B is defined as noble and refined belief, well organized, its spiritual world is more sincere and steady, seeking truth, goodness and beauty, playing god rather than the devil. Then "superstition" moves along the coordinate toward point A, and religion moves along the coordinate toward B. They move along the same coordinate and are mutually linked. But at the same time, they are different and they move in opposite directions. Because they move along the same coordinate, superstition may be confused with religion. Therefore, as we implement our policy of freedom of religious belief we must pay special attention never to grant freedom to the rampant spread of feudal superstition. When the National People's Congress examined the Ninth Five-year Plan and the Development Program for 2010, in finalizing the draft, a phrase was added intentionally at the suggestion of the delegates: "Do away with feudal superstition." That is indeed a complicated task that we must not ignore.

Why do we say that religious belief is an insistent spiritual pursuit, moving relatively toward sincerity (this is its essential difference from superstition)? Engels said: "All religions are nothing but reflections of the fantasy in people's mind of an external force controlling their daily life. In those reflections, human force assumes the form of a superhuman force."[164] As I see it, the "external force" that Engels mentioned in his first sentence means the objectively existing material for natural and social force, including both the "human force" mentioned in the second sentence, i.e., the material force that has been understood by man, and the "non-human force" not mentioned in that sentence, i.e., material force not yet understood by man. That the human force should assume "the form of superhuman force" as

---

[164] "Anti-Dubring," *Selected Works of Marx and Engels*, Volume III, p. 354.

"a reflection of fantasy" is undoubtedly an error in human thinking. But the reflection of fantasy about the material force that has not yet been understood is in fact a form in which human thinking seeks and explores the unknown world. For example, what is there in the depth of the universe? Before the Hubble telescope transmitted to earth the image of the Giant Eagle Nebula which is 400 million times further away from the sun, man inevitably engaged in fantasy. Therefore, we cannot say religion as a reflection of fantasy is simply stupidity or superstition. To be sure, we also cannot say it means the understanding of truth. What we are saying is merely that it is, to a certain extent a sincere and persistent spiritual pursuit, which has landed in the realm of error.

New species, sub-species, mutations and bogus species, and so on and so forth. We need to strengthen the administration of religious affairs. Do we have to strengthen the administration of these species? Generally speaking, they fall outside the business of the Bureau of Religious Affairs of the government. Who then is to take care of them? The religious circle is also critical of this. They say the government only controls the obedient, but does not control the disobedient. Each time control is strengthened, it would be "criticizing the late comers in the presence of those who have promptly arrived at the meeting," "no relaxation where relaxation is called for" and "no tightening where tightening is in order." These criticisms deserve our consideration.

In a word, the complexity of religion means that we need to recognize that religion itself is a system with very complex structures and functions. We also need to understand the diversity of the contradictions in religion, a very complex intertwining of prolonged evolution and sharp sudden change, contradictions among the people and contradictions between ourselves and the enemy, antagonistic and non-antagonistic contradictions, ideological faith and political stand, the national question and the religious question, the domestic question and the international question. We need to go deep into the realities of life, conduct investigations and research, make concrete analyses of specific questions, work hard to discard the dross and select the essential, eliminate the false and retain the true, moving from one point to another and from the superficial to the depth. We must not take a simple view of a complex problem, refrain from doing things in an oversimplified way for immediate pleasure, and thus create endless troubles for future work.

Are There Two Other Characteristics in Addition to the Five Characteristics?

The theory of the five characteristics makes a scientific generalization and helps us gain an overall understanding of religion and a penetrating knowledge of its characteristics. But when we assign them actual content in the light of actual conditions, and look at religion in the process of building the two civilizations, it seems possible to discuss two other characteristics in addition to the five characteristics.

Looking at religion in the process of the building of spiritual civilization, after we have strengthened the administration of religious affairs according to law, the harmony factor (*weiheti*) as an external element of religion and its links with the various aspects of social life are rather restricted in many ways. So the sentiment and knowledge — the internal elements of religion — and the latter's links with the ideological superstructure form the religious culture, which becomes rather active. In addition, religion must adapt itself to the building of socialist spiritual civilization so the cultural character of religion stands out. The venerable Zhao Puchu suggested that in addition to the five characteristics of religion, there is also the cultural character. This deserves consideration. In my view, efforts to support and guide the cultural, ethical, and philosophical tendencies of religion which raise the level of belief and avoid misleading the masses through its superstitious element are more beneficial than detrimental to the building of socialist civilization.

Looking at religion in the process of the building of material civilization, religion must adapt itself to real life, which centers on economic construction. So the secular character of religion stands out. Religion, which used to stress other worldliness, now strongly desire secularity. Examples are the "two world celebration" of Islam; the "solemn land and the happy profit" and "making a worldly career in an otherworldly spirit" of Buddhism; the "celebration of life" and "preservation of one's health" of Daoism; and "glorifying God and benefiting man" of Christianity. In addition to philanthropy, many religious organizations also run enterprises under the banner of "self-support." Sometimes we encounter people who are at once clergy and entrepreneur, who plunge into "the sea of (worldly) suffering" also "wet their feet in the sea of commerce." They are religionists of a new type. We need to study these new phenomena.

However, as the role of religion in the process of the building of the two civilizations is only beginning to show, whether we should really add the cultural and secular characteristics to the five analyzed above remains to be seen. Therefore, we generally refrain from talking about those two characteristics. It is better to consider them in the context of the "complex character."

Two Revelations
In the above, I tried to lend specific and actual contents to the "five characteristics" of religion in the light of the actual situation in China's religious question. This is not an attempt to be original, but an effort to apply the Marxist

view of religion in our new explorations of the new situation and new problems in religion. It is therefore difficult to avoid inaccuracies and imperfection, and revisions and additions will be made in the future. The above exposition is definitely not theorizing for its own sake, but an effort to provide a guide to our current work on religion. I believe there are two important revelations.

1. We insist that on upholding the three viewpoints — three barriers we must break through — in order to correctly understand and prudently handle China's current religious question.

The five characteristics of religion demand that in order to correctly understand and prudently handle China's current religious question, we must not neglect the three viewpoints, namely the political viewpoint, the mass viewpoint and the policy viewpoint Once these viewpoints are neglected, our view of the religious question will invariably be one-sided and erroneous. We will fail to reach the other side of the river of correct understanding. An erroneous understanding leads to erroneous conduct. Our work on religion will suffer unnecessary losses. It is therefore essential that we uphold the three viewpoints. It is like breaking through three barriers — our essential skill.

For example, we emphasize the political viewpoint. This means that we should look at the religious question from a political viewpoint. We should look at things to determine whether they benefit the reform, development and stability, and the long-term security and prosperity of the country. Religion has always performed a function either to stabilize or destabilize society. In that sense "no religious matter is a small matter." The correct handling of the religious question is of the utmost importance. In the coming fifteen years of key importance to our economic growth we must work hard to avoid the sharpening and explosion of the religious question. Our work on religion must provide the guarantee for the realization of the great blueprint of the entire party and people throughout the country for this and the next century. In those fifteen years, the religious question must not be allowed to interfere with our central task. For this purpose, we must crack down according to law on all activities that undermine social stability and interfere with economic construction. At the same time, we also need to make some appropriate compromises and concessions for the development of religion on the condition that the dignity of the law and the people's interests are not compromised. We must actively guide the religions so that they can adapt themselves to the socialist society. It is possible to put aside minor differences so as to seek common ground, and looking at it in a fundamental way, it is in our interest to do so. The difference in faith between the great majority of religious believers and ourselves is after all minor. And the objective of our common struggle and the desire for political unity, cooperation, and stability are major. On the basis of setting aside minor differences so as to seek common ground, we should try to attract as much as possible the religious believers to the great cause of rejuvenating China. With the fulfillment of their targets set for 2010 and the realization of the great rejuvenation of the Chinese nation, and with the enhancement of the people's material and spiritual civilization, and the gradual relaxation of the social contradictions, the negative role of religion will also be greatly reduced.

To emphasize the mass viewpoint means that we must recognize the fact that there are 100 million religious believers. These are the basic masses we must respect and rely on. We must never regard them as an alien force. We must understand that even those who have been deceived into taking part in disturbances or even get involved in the underground forces or become cult followers remain special masses with whom we must unite and whom we must educate and win over. We must never "push them over" to the other side, but must "pull them over" to our side. To be sure, we must also respect the freedom of an even greater number of people who are not religious believers. We must never forget to "use Marxist philosophy to criticize idealism (including theism), educate the masses, and especially the broad masses of young people in the scientific world outlook of dialectical materialism and historical materialism, and to step up the dissemination of the scientific and cultural knowledge about natural phenomena, social evolution and the life, birth, age, illness, and death as well as good or ill luck of man. That is one of the important tasks of our party on the propaganda front." We must not allow it to happen that "there are people preaching theism, but no one talks about atheism." Work on religion is a special kind of mass work. We need to acquire special skills for this special task and constantly improve the quality of our work. We often see work on religion but not mass work; we only see "Buddha" without seeing the "monks." Lenin long ago taught us: "we must be especially prudent in our fight against religious prejudices. In that struggle, much harm can be done if we hurt people's religious feelings. The struggle should be waged through propaganda and education. Going too far in that struggle can infuriate the masses. Such a struggle can deepen the division caused by religious faith. And our strength lies in unity."[165]

When we stress the viewpoint of policy, it means that in handling the religious question, we must not allow each to go his own way. The Central Committee has emphasized again and again that "all members of our party must clearly understand that our policy toward religion is by no means a temporary and expedient one. It is founded on the foundation of the scientific theory of Marxism-Leninism-Mao

---

[165] *Complete Works of Lenin*, second edition, Volume 35, p. 181.

Zedong Thought, a strategic design to achieve the objective of uniting with people of all nationalities throughout the country to work together to build China into a modernized socialist power." The respect for and protection of the freedom of religious belief is a long-term basic policy. In order to achieve unanimous correct understanding of that policy, we need dialectical thinking, tactical planning, administration according to law, and give positive guidance. Premier Zhou said: "On the one hand we are not for unprincipled unity. On the other hand, we must not lose contact with the broad masses. This is a policy question, not a tactical one." In the new historical period, our parry, persisting in integrating the Marxist view of religion with the actual conditions of Chinese religion, has formulated a whole set of basic viewpoints and basic policies for correctly treating and handling the religious question. It has blazed a correct trail for solving the religious question that bears Chinese characteristics. And this has become an integral part of Deng Xiaoping's theory for building socialism with Chinese characteristics. We must seriously learn in our practice in order to understand the Marxist view of religion and our party's policy toward religion, and to carry it out in an all-round, correct, and energetic way.

2. To uphold the correct orientation and principles in our work on religion, we must strictly abide by the three phrases.
     Comrade Jiang Zemin pointed out that we need to stress three phrases concerning the religious question: one is implementing the party's policy toward religion in an all-round and correct manner; two is strengthening the administering of religious affairs according to law; three is actively guiding the religions in such a way that they can adapt themselves to the socialist society. These three phrases were also stressed by Comrade Li Peng in his report to the Fourth Session of the Eighth National People's Congress. In short, we need to pay attention to policy, administration, and adaptation. This is the crystallization of the integration of the Marxist view of religion with the actual conditions in Chinese religion. The three phrases serve as the guidelines that must be followed in order successfully to perform our work on religion in the new period.
     These three phrases are rich in their contents. Basing ourselves on the relevant important documents, law and regulations, and important speeches made by leading comrades of the central authorities in the new period, we have worked out thirty major points. (See the article "Pay Attention to Policy, Administration and Adaptation" on the Theory Page of *People's Daily*, March 14, 1995). These major policy points reflect the all-round and profound grasp by our party of the five characteristics of religion and the laws governing religion itself. There are internal links between the three phrases that cannot be severed. The implementation of the

policy toward religion and the successful administration of religious affairs according to law are formulations from the policy and legal angles and are entirely consistent in essence. The central idea is that, in the process of handling the religious question, we must protect the legal, curb the illegal, crack down on violators, and administer religious affairs according to law. It is also the process of implementing the policy toward religion. But the two assume different forms. The law and regulations governing religion represent the institutionalization and codification of the policy toward religion. Administration according to law is coercive in nature. The purpose of all-round correct implementation of the policy toward religion, and of strengthening the administration of religious affairs according to law is actively to guide the religions to adapt themselves to the socialist society. A single principle is embodied in the three phrases, i.e., all-round and correct implementation of the party's policy toward religion. Special emphasis is on the key point: conscientiously strengthen the administration of religious affairs according to law with the aim of solving the problems in our current work on religion. We must aim at one target, i.e., guide the religions in such a way that they would adapt themselves to the socialist society. When we carry out the basic principle and stress the need to "pay attention to policy," when we emphasize the key point and stress the need to "pay attention to administration," when we talk about the purpose of our work and stress the need to "pay attention to adaptation," we stress one of the three phrases at a time. But the three phrases are in essence closely linked, and every one of them gives expression to all three of them. We must understand them as a single whole. That is the essence of understanding and grasping the party's policy toward religion in the new period. It gives expression to upholding the principle of seeking truth from facts, upholding dialectics and the cardinal principles and orientation. It would be an error in our understanding if we consider the policy of freedom of religious belief in isolation from the administration of religious affairs according to law or if we go so far as to pit one against the other. Then we will certainly err in our work. And if we carry out the policy and administer according to law but forget that our starting point and final purpose is to unite all religious believers with all non-believers in a common effort to build a modern socialist power, our work on religion would be without purpose and we would lose our bearings.

From the above, I hold that in order to correctly handle China's current religious question, it is very important that we make a serious analysis of the five characteristics of religion in the light of the actual situation in our current religious question and our work on religion, and that we apply the five-character theory to a description of the overall situation in religion so as to make some basic analyses of the law governing religion. When we look at a problem and perform our work,

Errata

we must pay attention to breaking through three barriers. We must abide by the three phrases, i.e., when we deal with religion, we need to analyze its five characteristics; when we deal with a problem, we need to break through the three barriers; and when we do our work, we need to carry out the three phrases.